"Tearing Open the Sleeping Soul"

Gregory the Great

This book contains transcripts, not reviewed by the authors, of talks given at the New York Encounter 2024

Crossroads Cultural Center

Human Adventure Books

Transcription & Layout
Deep River Media, LLC

Publisher
Human Adventure Books

All rights reserved. Printed in the United States of America. No part of this book may be used or reproduced in any manner whatsoever without written permission except in the case of brief quotations embodied in critical articles or reviews.

Tearing Open the Sleeping Soul
Proceedings of New York Encounter 2024
Crossroads Cultural Center
This edition © 2024 Human Adventure Books

Contents

A Soul Waiting to be Reawakened   9

The Power of Language   21

A Fundamental Difference?   37

A Torn Open Wound   51

Still Awake!   71

What Beauty Can Do to the Soul   85

Made to be Free   101

An Incurable Wound?   119

Beyond Left and Right   137

From Death Into Life   153

"Tearing Open the Sleeping Soul"

Gregory the Great

New York Encounter 2024

What is happening to our humanity?

There is no shortage of reasons to ponder this question: daily images of gratuitous violence; an epidemic of suicide; feeling suffocated by the imposition of opposite ideologies and their language, starting in school; the potential threat of generative AI; a sense of paralysis in front of the future; suffering and evil devoid of meaning or redemption; general weariness, malaise, numbness, and lack of desire.

These signs suggest that our humanity is asleep. What can reawaken it?

> "Something unexpected is the only hope."
> —Eugenio Montale, *Before the Trip*

When something wakes us up, things come alive again. If we pay attention to our experience, these very same signs reveal that what makes us human is irreducible. We are ill at ease with our apathy because we are made to desire. We feel lonely because we are made to be in relationship. We feel empty when we "check-out" because we are meant to be "checked-in." We feel disappointed because to be born comes with a promise. We are afraid because we have something to lose. We feel suffocated because we are made to be free and to affirm what is true. And we feel lost because we are made for a purpose.

"Childhood memories...tears of happiness...the bitterness of parting...a mother's tenderness...friendship...sudden hope...a fortunate guess...melancholy...unreasoning joy...The machine may be able to recreate all of this! But the surface of the whole earth would be too small to accommodate this machine."

—Vasily Grossman, *Life and Fate*

New York Encounter 2024

Tearing Open the Sleeping Soul

A Soul Waiting to be Reawakened

*The Encounter opens with poet **Christian Wiman** and classical pianist **Lio Kuok-Wai**.*

Introduction

"Expectation is the very structure of our nature, it is the essence of our soul. It is not something calculated: it is given. For the promise is at the origin, from the very origin of our creation. He who has made man has also made him as 'promise.' Structurally man awaits; structurally man is a beggar; structurally life is promise."
– Fr. Luigi Giussani, *The Religious Sense*, McGill-Queen's University Press, 2023, page 55.

In front of the daily images of wars and gratuitous violence, the epidemic of suicide, the suffocation of ideologies, and the sense of paralysis in front of the future, is this promise really the irreducible essence of our soul? Can it ever be fulfilled? Can it ever be eliminated or just ignored? This year's Encounter journey to explore these questions starts with poetry and music.

Christian Wiman: Good evening. *It's been a long time since the beat of my heart was a friend.* That's the line of that song that really stuck out for me. It reminds me of a Gerard Manley Hopkins poem that begins, "My own heart / let me more have pity on / Let me live to my sad self hereafter kind." That's a familiar sentiment and predicament to me and probably to a lot of you as well. The focus of this conference is how to have hope in the face of despair; specifically, how to wake up in such a way that we can remember what hope is, and what we are. No small part of the reason why consciousness turns inward and becomes corrosive is because we lose the sense of consciousness. There's a cumulative feeling right now of being overwhelmed. Is it all the political noise, the environmental and economic problems that have come to seem both intractable and crushing? The despair attendant to where we seem to be heading as a country, even as a species? Is it all of this put together? Blaise Pascal famously said that all the problems of the world could be traced back to our inability to just sit quietly with our own thoughts in a room for an hour. *It's been a long time since the beat of my heart was a friend.* How do we befriend the beating of our hearts? What if we can't even hear it?

Waking up — that's the first step. I'm struck by and completely agree with Fr. Giussani, his notion that Christianity is an event, and that precepts, doctrines, every last scrap of theology — this is all secondary. Why would anyone pursue God if they've never felt God? But we do lose faith with that feeling. It gets drowned out by cultural noise and simply the daily necessities of survival. The good news though, is that the event is not singular. It ramifies through every area of our lives, if we can just learn to listen. If you've ever lived in England, you know that on the radio, they have the shipping forecast. And it's a bit mysterious if you haven't ever experienced that. But that's how the poem ends. It's from Carol Ann Duffy and is called "Prayer."

> *Some days, although we cannot pray, a prayer*
> *utters itself. So, a woman will lift*
> *her head from the sieve of her hands and stare*
> *at the minims sung by a tree, a sudden gift.*
>
> *Some nights, although we are faithless, the truth*
> *enters our hearts, that small familiar pain;*
> *then a man will stand stock-still, hearing his youth*
> *in the distant Latin chanting of a train.*

A Soul Waiting to be Reawakened

Pray for us now. Grade 1 piano scales
console the lodger looking out across
a Midlands town. Then dusk, and someone calls
a child's name as though they named their loss.

Darkness outside. Inside, the radio's prayer —
Rockall. Malin. Dogger. Finisterre.

Faith comes through hearing. I always think of that line from the Apostle Paul when I read this prayer. Paul's talking about spreading the gospel, but as is often the case with scripture, some charged and less teachable truth has infiltrated the lesson. Faith comes in his deeper sense not through taking in and assimilating the meaning of words, not really through content at all, at least not primarily — it comes literally from the air. From sound. I would say it's pre-Christian, if Christianity didn't itself contain its own cosmic origin and extinction. *In the beginning was the Word and the Word was with God and the Word was God.* The origin because that verse puts Christ not simply at the beginning of creation but as its source and means of sustenance. Extinction, because every human utterance exists in the shadow of, and is annihilated in, the full light of that Divine One. You can't hear the word, the lowercase word of God, until you've heard the uppercase Word of God. The first is imparted, the second intuited. The lowercase word comes from a minister of whatever sort of poet is speaking to you at a conference, for instance. The uppercase Word might come from the leaves of a tree, or a rudimentary piano lesson, or a radio's shipping forecast. Sound, then, that's the first thing to attend to in poems, and what a sound that solemn sonnet makes. It's so beautiful, in fact, so consolingly clear and assured that you might not notice the enormous gulfs of despair and unbelief that it's carried you over. There's a sense of volatile melancholy in the poem. Is that woman with her head in her hands praying? Or is she grieving? It's a sorrow just on the verge of revelation.

The theologian Alexander Schmemann says the knowledge of the fallen world has not killed joy, which emanates in this world always constantly as a bright sorrow. And then that sorrow becomes more explicit. In the poem, someone calls a child's name, as though they named their loss. The pain of childhood, even if it's just the sense of its end, gets healed over by time until one day you find yourself with your own child, whose presence gives you so much joy that it jolts loose a sadness, a wound you'd forgotten, and you call your child's name as though you named your loss. The truth that enters our heart is restorative and necessary, but it's also a small, familiar pain. W.H. Auden once defined poetry as the clear expression of mixed feelings. The truth of this poem is small and familiar and deeply consoling. But it's also pain. "Prayer" ends with those place names from the shipping forecast as if the very earth cried out to God, as indeed it does sometimes in Scripture, which is precisely the point. Some days, although we cannot pray because we're too busy or because we're in too much pain, or simply because of the whole culture seems calcified around us, a prayer seems to utter itself.

There's a wrenching moment near the end of Marilyn Robinson's novel *Lila*, when the title character and her husband, John Ames, are discussing, even sort of arguing, issues of faith and prayer. And Ames finally throws up his arms and he says, *Family is a prayer, wife is a prayer, marriage is a prayer*. By which he means to say something similar to what Carol Ann Duffy is saying in that poem I just read: that the world and our soul, our existence and gods are far more permeable and much more possible than words like *faith*, *truth*, or even *prayer* can suggest. A poem can be one of those minor events that recalls the major one, it can shock consciousness awake to reality, and the consciousness that's truly awake to reality is awake to God. That can be a hard thing to realize and hold on to, though. We seem to never stop hungering after something that we can never quite name.

Some years ago, I wrote a whole book trying to answer the question, What is it that we want when we can't stop wanting? In that Carol Ann Duffy poem, the answer seems to be God. Freud thought the answer was death, an urge in organic life to restore an earlier state of things. The common answer of our own times is that there is no answer. It's all just nature. Genes rotely ramming home their mechanical codes one by one. We want because dissatisfaction equals survival. We are designed to improve and impart our hunger, breeding descendants with ever keener teeth. If we are conscious and honest, each of these answers will likely seem right at various times

A Soul Waiting to be Reawakened

in our lives. If we are conscious and honest, each of them at another time will seem wrong. As I was working on that book, I came across this quote by the theoretical physicist John Polkinghorne. "What gives continuity are not the atoms themselves, but the almost infinitely complex information-bearing pattern in which they are organized. The essence of this pattern is the soul. It will dissolve it death with the decay of the body, but it is a perfectly coherent belief that the faithful God will not allow it to be lost, that will preserve it in the divine memory."

That we might be remembered. What an almost impossible thought that is. That there's a consciousness capacious enough, merciful enough, to recall each of us in our entirety just as we recall our own fragile but meaningful moments. That our lives might be the Lord's insights.

Dietrich Bonhoeffer, just before his execution by the Nazis in 1945, wrote a surprising little poem that he put in the margin of something he was reading. "I demand my own life back / my past / you." That's not what you expect from someone who's confronting his own death. It's not the future that Bonhoeffer feels slipping from him but the past – he still believes in salvation – but its molecular singularity, all the minute perceptions and sensations retained by the body, if not the mind, that comprise one particular human consciousness. What is it we want when we can't stop wanting? "Lord," prays a character in Ilya Kaminsky's *Dancing in Odessa*, "give us what you have already given."

Twenty years ago I became the editor of *Poetry* magazine in Chicago, and the first official event over which I presided was a longstanding Chicago tradition called Poetry Day. That year it culminated with a large public reading by Mary Oliver, who at the time was easily the most famous poet in the country, though *famous poet* is maybe a hard phrase to utter without irony. Mark Strand once said it's like being famous in your family. Still, poets do tend to acquire outsize egos, and I was prepared to meet someone with a kind of impenetrable nimbus around her. Not so. I first saw her in the lobby of her downtown hotel, dressed for this upscale occasion in hiking boots, wrinkled chinos, and what appeared to be a hunting jacket a size too large. It looked like she might have cut her own hair. Her head was bent over a thick book that I saw as she rose was *The Faerie Queen*. My face must have registered some surprise. "I'm not young," she shrugged, as she opened her knapsack and exchanged Spencer for a pack of cigarettes. "I want to spend what time I have left with masterpieces." She meant it, too.

I saw her on a couple of other occasions that night, including right when we were sitting next to each other, and she was about to go on stage with that huge poem open, reading it. Mary was traveling alone because Molly, her partner for over 40 years, was already sick with the illness that would kill her. Not that Mary mentioned any of this to me; we talked to one thing and another and we were walking down Michigan Avenue when Mary suddenly stopped and picked up a piece of meat. At least that's what I thought it was. When she spread that gray red mess out on her hands, you could see that it was — or at least it had been — a bird. A pigeon, in fact, which she proceeded to describe with avid eyes and intelligent touch, showing me exactly where the hawk had struck, where the talons had clutched and torn, and she said that probably the hawk had dropped this half-eaten carcass into the crowd and wasn't able to recover it. We stood there for a minute. It's a huge reading. I'm getting nervous. I say, "Mary, we gotta go." And she takes that bird. She sticks it in her pocket.

She kept it with her all night. She kept it while she was giving the reading and she kept it during the party afterwards. And I know this because at one point we had both retreated to the kitchen and she took out that bird to show me something else that she had noticed: the sense of mortality — our own, of course, but also of those we most love. It doesn't cast us backward only, like Bonhoeffer wrote, it also propels the imagination forward and makes us imagine heavens in which wounds are healed and losses restored. Or to ameliorate oblivions by imagining our atoms alive and other forms, like Polkinghorne said. But Heaven too often turns out to be little more than projections of the precious self, *ad infinitum*. And it's a cold comfort to think of one's dear smithereens blasted through some new forms of matter from which we, whatever it is that makes us *us* — have vanished.

Here's Polkinghorne again. "Death is present in this world because of the Second Law of Thermodynamics, which says that in the end disorder always wins over order. However, it seems perfectly coherent to believe that God could bring into being a new kind of matter, with such strong self-organizing principles that the drift to disorder would no longer happen. Or perhaps that the notion of disorder would be naive. That we might be a form, or part of a form whose fruition for now we can intuit but not inhabit, that heaven and oblivion might have one name, which every poet in one way or another, is trying to speak."

This is a Mary Oliver poem.

> *Coming down*
> *out of the freezing sky*
> *with its depths of light,*
> *like an angel,*
> *or a buddha with wings,*
> *it was beautiful*
> *and accurate,*
> *striking the snow and whatever was there*
> *with a force that left the imprint*
> *of the tips of its wings –*
> *five feet apart – and the grabbing*
> *thrust of its feet,*
> *and the indentation of what had been running*
> *through the white valleys*
> *of the snow –*
>
> *and then it rose, gracefully,*
> *and flew back to the frozen marshes,*
> *to lurk there,*
> *like a little lighthouse,*
> *in the blue shadows –*
> *so I thought:*
> *maybe death*
> *isn't darkness, after all,*
> *but so much light*
> *wrapping itself around us –*
> *as soft as feathers –*

> *that we are instantly weary*
> *of looking, and looking, and shut our eyes,*
>
> *not without amazement,*
> *and let ourselves be carried,*
> *as through the translucence of mica,*
> *to the river*
> *that is without the least dapple or shadow –*
> *that is nothing but light – scalding, aortal light –*
> *in which we are washed and washed*
> *out of our bones.*

Why a poem about death when we're talking about trying to wake up to life? Because unconsciousness of death or wrong consciousness of death is often the very thing that keeps us from apprehending life. To be conscious is to be conscious of death, and you must figure out what right consciousness is in that regard. Fr. Giussani also once said that the proper spiritual life inheres in the development of a gaze, a right way of seeing.

Let me end with a poem that seems to me the best example of this. Osip Mandelstam was one of the greatest poets of the 20th century, one of the greatest minds of the 20th century. He died in 1938, when he was 47. He was last seen at a transit camp for political prisoners in Siberia, picking through a garbage heap for food. It was a situation that he had long foreseen and actually sort of precipitated in 1934. With incredible bravery and suicidal foolishness, Mandelstam recited at a literary gathering a poem that he just written, a very famous poem now known as the "Stalin Epigram." And it turned all the great leaders' pomp into a kind of puppet show. He compared his moustache to a cockroach, he said that he was a pig farmer. And of course, Stalin was very sensitive in that he thought of himself as an intellectual. Maybe Mandelstam believed he was among friends, though even friends had begun to watch their words by then. Maybe he believed in his own gift so utterly that he mistook imaginative freedom for actual freedom. Maybe he had the saintly sense not to credit safe distinctions between kinds of freedom. Men like Dietrich Bonhoeffer, before he left New York to return to his beloved and benighted Germany, did only what his own soul did him to do. And in any event, someone at that literary gathering in Moscow, someone whose memory was trained in just the way that Mandelstam's was and could recite a poem after hearing it only once, whispered it in the ear of one of Stalin's goons. And that was it. From Moscow to Leningrad to outer exile, Mandelstam and his wife lived on the move, subsisting on scraps and hope, on love and poetry. This is a tiny little poem:

Come love let us sit together
In the cramped kitchen breathing kerosene.
There's fuel enough to forget the weather,
The knife is ours and the bread is clean.

Come love let us play the game
Of what to take and when to run,
Of come with me and come what may
And holding hands to hold off the sun.

Probably though, the epigram only accelerated events that were inevitable. Stalin was absolutely obsessed with Mandelsta. It was the pure lyric spirit of him that Stalin couldn't abide, the existential liberty and largess. It's like a free singing soul that Stalin felt was the one thing that slipped through his nets. People who think poetry has no power have a very limited conception of what power means. Even now, in this corporate country where presidents don't call up poets on the phone, some little lyric is eating into the fat heart of money. But it's more than that. Poetry — all art — protects and sustains the consciousness that the blob seeks to erase, needs to erase if it's going to maintain power. one life, one mind, one instant responding to the minums sung by a tree, or the poem that lets you hear it — these things matter immensely, both in terms of preserving a spirit that's worth fighting for, and for fully sounding all the notes God means to sing. For I am convinced that every single one of us is part of some ultimate unity, an existential symphony of sorts. But we have to allow ourselves to be sounded, as it were, to discern what our particular note is. I will leave you with this one utterly true note, which is the last poem that Osip Mandelstam wrote. He was completely aware of the fate that bore down upon him, but he was still astonished at consciousness — both its gift and its cost.

> *And I was alive in the blizzard of the blossoming pear,*
> *Myself I stood in the storm of the bird-cherry tree.*
> *It was all leaflife and starshower, unerring, self-shattering power,*
> *And it was all aimed at me.*
>
> *What is this dire delight flowering fleeing always earth?*
> *What is being? What is truth?*
>
> *Blossoms rupture and rapture the air,*
> *All hover and hammer,*
> *Time intensified and time intolerable, sweetness raveling rot.*
> *It is now. It is not.*

Thank you. [*applause*]

Deniz Demirer: Beethoven's Fifth Piano Sonata in C Minor is a melancholic piece. Melancholy, sadness, are a clear and moving signal that being born for happiness is not a phenomenon that concerns just an individual person. It involves everyone and everyone's destiny. In the embrace of one's own heaviness, of one's own fatigue — at a certain point the horizon opens up and everything takes on a lightness. Toil, pain, and physical suffering are not taken away, but one feels happy because he's supported, sustained, helped, loved.

The itinerary traced out by the three movements of the Sonata is the same. In the end, the limitation of things is transfigured. And in the limitation itself we have already an anticipation and a foretaste of the Unlimited, almost a twilight, almost a dawn that is not yet here, but is already present. Within the ultimately still blind horizon of our experiences men, there is already this vanishing point. And what reality is a sign of enters into the sign and touches us, urges us, and says to us, "Let's go together."

Lio Kuok-Wai sits at his piano and plays the Sonata.
Afterwards, applause.

The Power of Language

A presentation on the nature of language and the danger of ideologies with **Andrea Moro**, *professor of general linguistics at the Institute of Advanced Studies, Pavia, Italy, and* **Marguerite Peeters**, *director of the Institute for Intercultural Dialogue Dynamics, Brussels. Moderated by* **Stephen Lewis**, *professor of English, Franciscan University of Steubenville.*

Introduction

Language is currently in the spotlight. Apart from the challenges posed by generative artificial intelligence and the need to identify what is uniquely human, language is being increasingly manipulated to influence or even create or impose a certain worldview. Dr. Moro will first address how language is a defining feature of our human identity and is intrinsically connected to how we experience reality. Dr. Peeters will then show how changing the vocabulary can have a profound impact, greater than we normally think, on how we relate to people and things. She will also address how a certain ideological use of language has evolved in the last decades and why.

Stephen Lewis, moderator: Good morning everyone. On behalf of the Encounter, I want to welcome everybody, both those here at the Metropolitan Pavilion and those that are watching us online. My name is Steven Lewis. I'm a professor of English at the Franciscan University of Steubenville, and

I will be the moderator for this event. I'm going to give a shortened bio for each speaker — the longer bios are available in the program.

Andrea Morrow is professor of general linguistics at the School of Advanced Studies in Pavia, Italy. He obtained a PhD in linguistics at the University of Padua. He has been a visiting scientist several times at MIT, first with a Fulbright grant. And then at Harvard. He studies the structure of human languages and their relationship with the brain. He is the author of several books published by MIT Press, including *Impossible Languages*, in 2016. *The Secrets of Words*, which he wrote with Noam Chomsky in 2022. And most recently a novel, *The Secret of Pietramala*.

Marguerite Peters is the director of Dialogue Dynamics, a Brussels-based institute studying the key concepts and operational mechanisms of globalization, with a view to promoting an intercultural dialogue on such issues. Marguerite holds a PhD in Political Science from the Wyszyński University in Warsaw, Poland. Her books, which have ben translated into a number of languages, include *The Globalization of the Western Cultural Revolution*. So let's welcome our speakers. [*applause*] Andrea will begin.

Andrea Moro: Okay, so let me start at the top. Thank you for the presentation. And thank you all for being here. In this warm morning, let me start with a kind of a methodological principle that I would like you to have in the back of your mind throughout this presentation, which is the idea that sometimes to explain what is possible, one must first capture what is *im*possible. Now before starting, I organize this talk in four steps. And I hope to be able to get you through this trip between grammar and brain. If you come out of this room with more answers than questions, then I failed; if you have more questions, then I will be very happy.

Let me start with the idea of information, which incidentally has an extremely interesting etymology. Information in first approximation can be considered the trace or the world of an individual. All animals receive units of information and selectively store them into their brain. [*He points at a PowerPoint slide on the screen*] What you see there actually is a stone and a frog's brain. In a sense, a frog's brain and a stone are quite similar at the level of complexity and elaboration of information. And then humans come. Humans also store experience in their brains as a finite set of words.

The Power of Language

But it can also generate new and potentially infinite representations by recombining the very same words in different order. And this is what is called *syntax*. Let me give you a micro language made only in three words, a verb, a name and another name. A human brain, with these three words, can construct two completely different scenarios. Cain killed Abel; Abel killed Cain. Same bricks, different structure, different meaning. This is what is called syntax. Interestingly enough, syntax is independent of meaning. Why is it so, because it's actually kind of counterintuitive, no? Well, we can say this triangle is blue, and that makes sense. We can think of a blue triangle. But actually, we can say this triangle is a circle, which is impossible to figure out even if you think a lot. Some of my students come up at the end of the class and say they've figured out the circle triangle problem [*audience laughter*], but believe me, it should be impossible. What is also impossible, strangely enough, is that you can create words and create fake vocabularies and say something like, "The goal of gum for the brows," which I hope doesn't mean anything. But this is actually something that humans have always done. If you see the Voynich manuscript at Yale, which invented plants, which is a wonderful piece of art, you wouldrecognize that in all literature, and even in children's plays, everyone invents words, from the Jabberwocky up to the Italian Fosco Maraini.

But then comes the real striking fact. As I told you, a frog and a stone can incorporate information from the outside. So suppose we are seeing the following scene: a girl saw a rose-shaped clouds over the hill. And then you perhaps experience another phenomenon and say, "A boy heard a dog barking in a dark forest." We take these two sentences that correspond to an experience. And you we come up saying, "A dog saw a dark rose barking over the cloud." This is human: by recombining words, we can describe things that never happened. And this is the crucial fact implied by syntax. We can generate meanings that do not correspond to any experience. This is sometimes called a "creative use of syntax," or in short, *fantasy*. Syntax is the boundary between all animals and us. This was recognized by Descartes: "There exists no person who cannot put together words, and by this compose a discourse to express his thoughts. On the contrary, there is no other animal so perfect or posed in such a favorable condition to perform the same task." Four hundred years later, Steven Anderson, the President of the American linguistic Society, said essentially the same thing: "The communication systems of all known animals are based on limited, fixed sets of discrete messages, and one that cannot be expanded by combining elements to form new and different complex messages." Now, the question could be, Are we sure? Are we sure that there is no animal that can do that? Well, actually here in New York, in the 1970s, a wonderful experiment was carried out by Thomas Bevere, now at the University of Arizona in Tucson, and Laura Petitto, a Canadian woman. They taught sign language to a chimp. You know, chimps have no less than 98% of our genome. And it was very interesting. This is the paper which came out in *Science*. [*points to the screen*] And this is a picture of Laura with Nim Chimpsky – that was the name of the chimp. And the chimp was able to learn 128 different words! Well, when it came to combining words to get meaning, none of 19,000 sentences or sequences was meaningful. So chimps have dictionaries but they don't have syntax.

Our brain is unique in that we can compose meaning by recombining the same bricks and get to something that was completely unexpected. There was a myth that survived up until the '50s, which can be summarized with the following quotation. "Languages can differ from each other without limits, and in unpredictable ways." Martin Joos, 1957. And then things have been completely revolutionized by applying to syntax the same thing that was applied to all other domains of science, like physics. The idea was that you can basically take a complex thing and reduce it to simple animals and simple operations. This is called deconstruction. Deconstruction of synthetic complexes into simple units and operations started in the '50s at MIT by Noam Chomsky, who proved that there are limits to variation in all languages, provided by the same core set of principles. Other extremely important work was done by Joseph Greenberg, who compared different languages.

Now, this is a delicate slide, because I want to convince you, I want to give you at least an image of what the decomposition means. I found an object, a piece of art – I was in New York, like I was 20 years old. It was at the Metropolitan Museum; I'll show you the the piece of art. The first thing you will see is chaos. But by the end of the image, you will see what it means. It is a sculpture by Man Ray, who built it in 1920. Look, it's called "Obstruction." It's 63 coathangers, projecting a chaotic shadow over a surface. The shadow is completely chaotic. The shadow is human grammars. All languages look chaotic. And in fact, as adults, when we want to learn a different language we find ourself in, you know, in a jungle, in a forest of rules, but actually, everything seen from that point of view is simple. And the path that the linguists have to take is to go up and see the simple object and the simple rules. Sometimes I use the example of a tapestry. You know, if you look at the tapestry from one side, you see all the dots. But if you do something you shouldn't do in museums and you go and see the other side, you see that perhaps two red dots are the same wire that goes back and hides. Grammar is this.

I hate when speakers only make allusions. So I want to give you one simple but core example that can give you an idea of how things works. Let's take from the dictionary a proper noun, a proper name, *Tim*. And think of it as a box, where boxes come in different sizes. You can put a box within another box. Then I go back to the dictionary and I take another word like *uncles*, and I can say, "The uncles of Tim" – a box in a box. And then I can do that another time. I could say, "The friends of the uncles of Tim." In natural languages, words are grouped as if they were nested in potentially infinite boxes. This is technically called *syntactic recursion*.

Well, now we are ready to give a recipe for an impossible language. Let's take a very, very simple rule that happens to be real in English and in many Indo-European languages, though not exemplified in Asian languages. Still, we could give another example that works in Asian languages too. The simple rule is to have in mind the subject-predicate agreement in clause structure. It's very simple. Take the dictionary and extract a word, *Mary*, and a verb like *run*. You put them together, they react, and they form a clause. The symptom that the clause works is agreement. So you say, "Mary runs." That's the way our brain works. The noun precedes the verb. Now, instead of taking *Mary*, let's take a larger box with *The friends of Mary*. And the only possible sentence becomes, "The friends of Mary run." Mary becomes invisible to the verb. The only thing we can have is agreement of *run* with a plural *friends*. This is done by instinct. We don't have to reason about that.

The generalization, which is very interesting, is that synthetic rules are based on nesting and not on the linear order of words. Well, the discovery of all this in the second half of the 20th century was that more generally, comparative syntax proves that, with no exception, rules never follow linear order. Linear order is the only physical requirement a language has.

Now let's turn to the third part, which is a core part of today's communication. There is an immediate question that can be posed. What are the boundaries of Babel generated by? Where do they come from? Actually, we have two options, which are exactly the same options that Plato had: nature or nurture. I want to read you sentence from a wonderful book, *The Biological Foundations of Language* by Eric Lenneberg. Lenneberg was a neuropsychologist at Massachusetts General Hospital, who discovered that when a patient had aphasia due to a brain tumor, or any kind of infection – if it happened before puberty, then recovery was 90% possible. After puberty, however, it was not. It couldn't be the case that this is all cultural. In the introduction to his book he says something extremely important, because sometimes ideology is what prevents science from taking the necessary steps. Here's the thing: a biological investigation into language must seem paradoxical, as it is so widely assumed that language consists of arbitrary cultural conventions, like language is a totally arbitrary set of rules. If languages are limited by our neurobiological architecture instead of culture, rather than by cultural conversion artifacts, then there must be such things as impossible languages, namely, coherent, even simpler structures, which are not recognized as languages by our brain. It's like eating. Humans can eat very different things: only vegetables, only meat, insects. I live in Pavia, in northern Italy. We eat mosquitoes, which were invented in Pavia in the 17th century. [*audience laughter*] But we never drink gasoline; it's not a cultural thing. We're simply not designed to drink gasoline. So I want to show you that we could construct a gasoline grammar, something that our brain is unable to digest.

An experiment was done twice. I wanted to do it with two different teams. First, a group of monolingual German speakers were taught a micro Italian and micro Japanese, including possible and impossible rules. Second, a group of Italian speakers were exposed to an invented lexicon language and included both possible and impossible rules with no explicit instructions. And then here's the core slide. We used fMRI. fMRI machines are not intelligent, not smart. They are machines, like scissors like microscopes. But they can be very useful in this case. They can highlight the network in the brain that is involved in doing a certain task. We explored the activation of Broca's Area, something that in all right-handed people and 70% of left handed people is activated while doing linguistic tasks with syntax. We measured accuracy. The subject had a series of sentences and had to say whether the rule was applied correctly or incorrectly. And then we measured the amount of blood in Broca's Area. First result was with possible rules. The result was as expected: more accuracy, more blood. This means the brain recognized them. But with impossible rules, something happened, which was exactly what everyone expected and hoped for in the experiment — namely, the opposite. The more they could manage with impossible rules, the less that economical structure was activated. The activation of Broca's Area rose when the accuracy of possible rules increased, but it diminished when the accuracy of impossible rules increased. There was no instruction at all. In a nutshell, the idea is that these limits help children to learn a language.

Let me go to the fourth path. We were interested in the distinction between humans and animals. And now there is a third protagonist in the scenario, which is machines. Let me read something that was written in the 1970s, describing what was happening at MIT in the 1950s. This description is by Joshua Hillel, a great philosopher and logician. There was a ubiquitous and overwhelming feeling around the laboratory at MIT regarding the new insights of cybernetics and the newly developed techniques of information theory. Now, substitute *cybernetic* with *AI* and you see we are at the same point today. We have thrown out humans from the scenario. Where are we? Again, several paths depart from here, but I want to show you one single thing, namely, a test and experiment that we ran. You consciously take a simple sentence in English like, *You think I must judge the nurse before meeting the doctor.* I want to teach you how to make interrogative sentence, so now you can say, *Which nurse do you think I must judge before meeting a doctor?* Which is a perfectly good English sentence. And now I aske you, *Which doctor do you think I must judge a nurse before meeting?* I mean, I can sort of figure out what you're asking, but but that's not the way you do that. The ungrammaticality of the third sentence doesn't follow from any reason. There is a purely geometric explanation based on hierarchical structure, which holds in all languages. And now the point: I went to ChatGPT, and I asked, *Which nurse do you think I should evaluate before meeting the doctor?* ChatGPT was kind of offended and told me if you're looking to evaluate, you know, a nurse before meeting the doctor, you may want to consider consulting with the nurse's direct supervisor in blah, blah, blah. So then I asked ChatGPT, *Which doctor do you think I should evaluate the nurse before meeting anytime soon?* And it responded, *You're looking to evaluate the nurse's clinical knowledge and blah, blah, blah.* ChatGPT responded to the question formulated with impossible rules and thus showed that it had no limit, no limit at all.

So there is a general conclusion we can make of this. Machines were thought to be too weak to compete with humans, but it turned out that they are too powerful to be compared to us. We evolved with limits that may not be rational, nevertheless the limits have allowed us to evolve the rational mind and attempt to capture aspects of reality.

There is something that I learned many years ago at the Rimini Meeting when Owen Gingrich was invited to give a wonderful talk about Galileo. If we think of objects falling, we are instinctively led to think that heavier objects falls faster. But it's wrong. Galileo showed that it is, in fact, the other way around. Nevertheless, we have evolved the rational mind with the wrong limits, and we don't know why. Because in fact, we are our limits.

Let me give you the final slide. There is someone who influenced me a lot – Umberto Eco. He was mimicking Wittgenstein's motto and said, "Wherof one cannot theorize, thereof one must narrate." And this is why, since I could not teach a group of children an impossible language, I wrote a novel where people do this very thing. And strangely enough, they do it in the Upper West Side here in New York. And the book is *The Secret of Pietramala*. Let me thank you for your attention here. [*audience applause*]

Lewis: Thank you very much. We'll now hear from Marguerite Peeters.

Marguerite Peeters: Good morning, everyone. What a wonderful theme for this Encounter. Language has the power either to awaken us as human persons and fulfill its universal function, or to manipulate and enslave us. It is then at the service of ideological agendas and even of totalitarian regimes, as we have seen in communist times. As I speak here now, you and I are engaging our reason, our conscience, our heart, we are awake as free responsible persons. Are you awake? [*audience responds Yes*] But are you awake as free persons, as human persons? [*audience silence*] No answer? I commit to transmit to you what I hold to be true. And you are discerning whether what I'm saying is real, helpful, and conducive to happiness. Human language creates a bond of trust between human persons. In natural languages, there is a nexus between the word *reality* and truth. And as Andrea Moro just told us, there is a nexus between language and human identity. I would say also, there is a nexus between speech and love, at least love for the content that I am communicating, for out of the abundance of the heart the mouth speaks, but also hopefully, love for the truth and love for the person that I am speaking or listening to. I am not a chatbot, you are not automatons, we are not data fodder for algorithms. Some claim that we have entered a post-truth society, a society in which our emotions and individual choices matter more than reality, in which people are in practice no longer interested in the truth, in which my truth is not your truth, in which virtual reality is on a par with actual reality, in which social networks spread fake news. When the fundamental nexus between language and truth no longer exists, language can be manipulated at will. It then stops being an instrument of communication between people and becomes one of social division and chaos. The Latin word *communicatio* means to make common. The post-truth society is divisive. It turns reality into a text to be interpreted, a process of change deprived of fixed and substantial content. How did we come to this? If you read the Universal Declaration of Human Rights, you see that it does nothing more than declare what all women and men endowed with reason and conscience can universally recognize as true and good as belonging to our irreducible human nature. The language of the Declaration names reality as it is, it uses terms such as human person, inherent dignity, inalienable rights, spouse, motherhood, human personality, freedom of conscience, worship, authority of government, nations, the family based on marriage between a man and a woman, and recognized to be the natural and fundamental group unit of society. Since 1948, this universal language has either been reinterpreted or cancelled, sidelined, or substituted by a novel language. There has been a quiet semantic revolution.

Linguistics, the scientific study of language, has historically played a critical role in the advent of the of the post-truth era. Without entering into an analysis of the history of linguistics since the late 19th century, it is useful for our purposes to underline a trend in linguistics that has at once been foundationally dominant and ideological. At the beginning of the 20th century, the Swiss structuralist, Ferninand de Saussure, inventor of semiotics and the founder of linguistics, related meaning exclusively to the contrast between the abstract signs and words constituting language. He studied language in an auto referential way. He disconnected words from the concrete reality they were supposed to signify. In the late 1940s, Arnie Naess, the Norwegian philosopher who would later coin the deep ecology concept, developed a theory about semantic fluidity and vagueness. Any given utterance can be variously interpreted depending on context and circumstances, he stated. In the late 1960s, the French philosopher Jacques Derrida, a post-structuralist, believed deconstruction was happening pervasively in the United States, in all fields of human activity, whether it be cooking, architecture, geopolitics, law or the economy. He elaborated his deconstruction discourse, whereby he disconnected concepts, words, the substance. For him, meaning is never fixed. For Judith Butler, the famous author of *Gender Trouble*, this course is all there is, there is no reality, only representation. The American philosopher Richard Rorty affirmed that truths were human constructs, that knowledge was solely a linguistic affair.

So you see that in less than one century, these linguists and philosophers went from disconnecting words from reality to proclaiming that truth simply does not exist. These academics broke from Aristotle's metaphysical perspective. Faithfulness to reality has been a pillar of Western Civilization. The post-truth society denies reason the capacity to attain the truth.

We realize, dear friends, that this denial stems from a moral decision to say no to the truth. It stems from a will to liberate the human being from the constraints of reality, from the conditions of existence in which he or she was placed. No one better expressed such a rebellious will than Jean-Paul Sartre, the massively influential French philosopher who claimed that man had to free himself from what is so that he could live for himself.

This Western flight from reality has complex origins. One of them, I believe, is how Sigmund Freud, the immensely influential father of psychoanalysis, depicted a negative view of reality by opposing it to pleasure. Freud considered reality to be repressive of our sexual drives. Equally repressive in his view were what he called the superego, authority, the Father, norms, institutions, civilization, the moral conscience, God.

Herbert Marcuse, a libertarian follower of Freud, advocated in his book *Eros and Civilization*, the advent of a non-repressive society, a society in which our sexual drives would become cultural and political values. Western culture deducted from Freud's repressive view of reality that the way to liberation would go through the cultural murder of the Father, which was, as we know, a dominant theme of May '68. The rejection of authority manifested itself in all fields in politics. To give but one example, in the 1960s, the American political scientist, James Rosenau, coined the governance term, which has been in vogue ever since, and suggests the idea of an informal conceptual management process. In certain ways, governance deconstructs the authority of hard government, and in fact promotes a type of power deprived of authority – dangerous business. The non-repressive society has indeed come about since the 1960s. And with it, this aversive instrumentalisation of language for outright negation purposes, a new language emerged, expressing a deconstruction of everything that the May '68 generation wanted to liberate itself from: partners instead of spouses free love instead of marital commitment, free choice instead of moral conscience, couples and individuals instead of parents, families instead of the family, nature or the earth instead of creation, individual instead of person, and so on.

Now, the advocates of the gender agenda wish to free humanity even from the very categories of man and woman, father and mother, spouse, son and daughter, masculinity and femininity, complementarity between the sexes, the marriage and family institutions, our sexually differentiated bodies — which they claim would all be social constructs or stereotypes, contrary to civic equality and liberty, and therefore to be deconstructed by all means. The deconstruction of reality has notably taken place through the construction of a new language, an impressively ever-expanding panoply of new terms proper to the agenda revolution. Terms that do not name reality, but name the free choices of individuals seeking to free themselves from reality. Cis, nonbinary, drag queen, trans, third gender, external gender, bisexual, asexual, polyamorous, aromantic, etc. Lexicons proliferate in all areas to guide us through the maze of the new semantic systems.

What is really at stake here is our universal human identity. The revolution I am describing considers it the ultimate liberty to create oneself in a Promethean fashion, as if we had not received our being from another, as if we had not been engendered by a Father. This was already a Nietzschean idea. Judith Butler used the phrase "performative language" to describe how one allegedly becomes what one says and does, as if nothing would pre-exist one's word and deed. But an individual saying, "Let me be queer" cannot come to being out of nothing and exist as queer. That individual inevitably pre-exists as man or woman, his or her own word and volition. David Halperin, a queer theorist, called the queer identity an identity without an essence. Indeed, gender neutral pronouns refer to generic individuals. But isn't the identity of a citizen emptied from who he or she is an identity of one's own ever-changeable choosing? Clearly this is a dead end for humanity. Post-humanity seems to be the horizon, following this demolition enterprise.

Already in 1943, in his book *Being and Nothingness*, Sartre had come to the conclusion that man was a useless passion. Evolutions in the field of art since the beginning of the 20th century illustrate the deconstruction/reconstruction process of the Western cultural revolution, its effort to liberate us from reality and truth. After assimilating deconstruction with creation, destroying representation, absolutizing art that is separating art from any objective criteria of beauty, the revolutionary process has ultimately ushered in since the 1960s the proclamation that whatever the art is, whatever declares itself to be art, is art.

Dear friends, we have now got it. The freedom to choose is the cornerstone of the posttruth edifice. Traveling from one choice to the next has been the postmodern individual's way of life. Traveling expresses a decision to shun personal commitment to play one's life. The postmodern culture celebrates perpetual change. Human dignity, love, liberty, equality, universal human rights, democracy – are now subjected to an open-ended diversity of interpretive choices. The right to die with dignity means the right to choose euthanasia, and radically destabilizes the meaning of dignity. Words are willingly no longer defined, to leave room for all interpretative choices. Even a candidate to the Supreme Court could not, or refused to, define what a woman is. Maybe Humpty Dumpty could not. I'm sorry. Maybe Humpty Dumpty was an early precursor of our postmodern culture, when he famously declared when I use the word, it means just what I choose it to mean, neither more nor less. The problem is that the coexistence of substantially contradictory interpretations is not sustainable. There always ends up being a winner and a loser amidst a diversity of interpretations vying for semantic dominance.

The new system is not as inclusive as it pretends to be. Some are seeking to hegemonically impose a single interpretation as globally normative, to use semantic fog as a power grab strategy. They present the post-truth agenda as consensual, as common sense, to use an expression of Antonio Gramsci, as the new self-evident, meant to substitute what had been proclaimed to be self-evident in the US Declaration of Independence, the law of nature, open to the law written on our hearts, as understood in the biblical tradition. And in many respects, corresponding to the concept of universality in the Universal Declaration, one can only consent – also a Gramscian concept – to what is self-evident. But passively consenting to agendas forged by others has an anesthetic effect, it puts us to sleep. What we want to do here is to wake up. So, let us wake up to who we are as human persons, human persons made for love and for the truth, as human persons endowed with reason, conscience and heart. We are not constructed, we are not generated by algorithms, we are lovingly engendered. The starting point of the post-truth era was the cultural murder of the Father. St. John reveals to us that the word of God through whom all things came to be is the very Son of God. By culturally killing the Father, we separated ourselves from the One who engendered the Word. So let us go back to the Father, the source of language. Thank you. [*audience applause*]

Lewis: Thank you very much. We only have a couple of minutes. But there's one question that just seems to really stand out here. So both of these presentations are focused in different ways on limits to the arbitrary and on limits being part of being human. And yet Andrea is coming from a scientific point of view and Marguerite from very much a philosophical point of view. How can the two speak to each other? What sort of synthesis is perhaps emerging in this post-truth era, that Marguerite was was identifying?

Moro: First, a kind of general observation. I don't think that the boundary between science and philosophy is a true one. I mean, every single step we take, when we make an experiment, even a quantitative experiment, it is rooted in a precise philosophical attitude. I think that you got it, you synthesize it right. In both domains, we have to realize that reality comes first and reality has limits in it. One cannot deny the fact that interpretation cannot change. Reality is the object that commands it.

Peeters: Exactly. I think we need to really come back to who we are, to rediscover this sense of reality. I think this is the greatest challenge for our era in the time of virtual reality and artificial intelligence. To rediscover our humanity.

Moro: There was something you said when you were talking about the fact that people substitute the term nature to creation. That really struck me, because by insisting by canceling the term creator, we are actually wiping out the fact that certain facts in life are just a consequence of a willingness. When we ask who we are, we can't exclude the someone wanted us, individually and collectively. And I completely agree with you. This is a subtle but dangerous falsification of the process.

Lewis: Both Andrea and Marguerite will be available for book signing out there in the lobby. And Andrea has *The Secret of Words* and also *Impossible Languages* available, and Marguerite has *The Globalization of* *the Western Cultural Revolution*, so please visit them and have them sign copies of their books. One important announcement: you are a part of the New York Encounter, a place that welcomes everybody. Help us keep it alive. We invite you to give generously at our donation table outside this auditorium or in a couple of clicks at www.newyorkencounter.org/donate. Your donation is tax-deductible. So please join me in thanking our speakers one last time. [*audience applause*]

A Fundamental Difference?

*A conversation on generative artificial intelligence and its foreseeable development, with **Jon Stokes**, co-founder and chief product officer at Symbolic AI, and **Jennifer Strong**, audio journalist and executive producer of Shift. Moderated by **Davide Bolchini**, executive associate dean, Luddy School of Informatics, Indiana University.*

Introduction

The surprising rapid development of generative artificial intelligence has sparked excitement and generated concerns about possible negative impacts. It has also raised a more fundamental question about what, if any, distinguishes us from the machines we have created. Is there an absolute, qualitative difference between human and artificial Intelligence?

Davide Bolchini, moderator: Welcome to everybody, those who are here at the Pavilion and those following us online. My name is Davide Bolchini. I'm the Executive Associate Dean at the Luddy School of Informatics, Computing and Engineering at Indiana University, and I will moderate this event. We are grateful to have two distinguished guests today, which I will introduce briefly.

John Stokes is a cofounder and chief product officer at Symbolic AI, a company that builds AI power tools for publishers. He also writes about AI at *www.JohnStokes.com*. John is a software engineer and former CTO and is one of the cofounders of Arstechnica. Also, he has written a popular book on microprocessor architecture. Thank you for being with us.

Jennifer strong is the creator of several top science and tech podcasts that include *ProPublica*, *The Wall Street Journal*, and *MIT Technology Review*. Her latest show, *Shift*, was launched in 2023 and is distributed by Public Radio's PRX. She's been a keynote stage host and moderator at the United Nations General Assembly, South by Southwest, Web Summit, MTech, AI for Google Global Summit, the Future of Everything Festival, and many others. Thank you for being here.

The topic of artificial intelligence has been center stage at the Encounter for many years, because it has really become part of the fabric of our lives. When we search for the New York Encounter program on Google, when we navigate New York City on Google Maps, when we use social media, we are very well aware that AI engines are filtering for us lots of information among the sea of content that is out there, and it is already becoming part of how we interact with content and with people.

But recently, the development of generative AI engines and platforms like ChatGPT or Stable Diffusion has really started to put on the front stage the possibility that these tools can create things, create content, generate content that we ourselves used to create. And so the question is, What's the difference between what these engines do and create and what *we* create, what *we* can generate. Is there a fundamental difference between the nature of this engine, of these tools, and how we approach the creative act, how we approach our work? And so to explore some of these questions, just to set the stage, I would ask very briefly, John, maybe to introduce what you do and how your current work intersects with the latest development of AI.

John Stokes: I work with journalists and professional communicators. And the idea is that you bring your own notes, your own thoughts, your own notions, and you put them into generative AI, and AI actually pieces out the language and gives you this text artifact back that substantially represents what you intended to say, but you didn't actually type it out. And so I use retrieval, augmented generation for this. I use large language models. I spend a lot of time with embeddings and thinking about, you know, search, relevance, stuff like this. Also, deploying large language models. And so this is what I spend most of my engineering effort and most of my brain power on. I'm lucky that I get to work with expert users of language, editors and other writers, and, you know, I myself am an editor and a writer. We're able to evaluate the results of generative AI in detail and, in some cases, live on the web, where the piece goes out and then readers interact with it. You can sort of feel the limits of these models, not just in an abstract benchmark way, but, you know, in a way where people are trying to relate to them as as an attempt to communicate.

Bolchini: Jennifer, as a journalist, can you tell us how your work intersects with this latest generative AI development?

Jennifer Strong: I studied politics, history, religion, I studied the things that I thought would help me with journalism. I went into this field in the 1990s, so I've been doing this for a little while. Around 2016 or 2017, I made a pivot from covering the intersection of public policy and impacts on society — to covering what we call frontier technologies, technologies that people, most people, haven't really heard of yet. Synthetic biology applications, things like that. AI, crypto, various other things. I've had the great privilege to go in a experimental fighter plane and look at how AI is being used to train next generation Top Gun pilots. I've had the opportunity to go and see a lot of things. If somebody thinks I'm being pessimistic, call me out on it, because I don't mean to, but I do think that I tend to be a little grounded in what I think of as facts, what's really happening. Thank you.

Bolchini: So many people these days are experimenting with generative AI. One year ago we were talking with the Encounter organizer and some friends about hiw I, working in academia already, was receiving emails from students that used ChatGPT to send me emails. And people asked, How do you know if they've used AI? How do you know who wrote the essays and emails? Generative AI is changing the way we work, but oftentimes we don't have a clear understanding of what these engines do and how they work, right? And so I want to ask John: From your perspective as a software engineer, maybe you can offer a simple explanation to help us peek under the hood the generative AI engine. How do they do what they do? How?

Stokes: All right, that was a real question. I'm a little bit of a Platonist about this, and I can give an explanation that I think is useful, but there is much disagreement about what these things do, and this was when I first started to go back into this technology in 2021 and talk to researchers. This was a little shocking to me, because I saw them trying to grasp what the model was doing and try to theorize and reason about it in a way that was, like, basically philosophical. They were clearly confused. It's amazing, because they're present at the origin of this. They wrote the code that does this, and despite being a witness to the birth of it, we still don't understand it, and we have trouble even describing what a good explanation would look like at some useful level of abstraction, right? I can concoct it like in *Timaeus*; you know, I can say maybe this is a likely story of how this works. But I confess it's just a likely story. So the likely story that I would give is to say that generative AI is a way of letting us use computers to discover numbers that to us as humans are interesting, are useful, are meaningful.

It sounds like not that useful of an explanation, but if you think about it, every digital file is a number. This picture behind me is a number. It's just a large binary number on a disk somewhere, and we decode it through a codec, and it translates into something that seems meaningful to us.

Somewhere, on a hard drive, somewhere is a copy of Dune Two, which is to be released soon. It's a large number, that film on the disk. That number is also on the number line. There's a bit of a question whether the numbers preexist us, like we speak of the search for primes. Somebody searches for a new prime number. I'm hunting for something that already exists. There's the great internet Mersenne prime search, which is, everybody gets their computers together and they all run through these algorithms and they try to find a new prime, as if this prime number existed on the number line. And then I applied computers to the process of discovering this prime number.

I want to suggest that there's a copy of Dune Two on the number line somewhere, where all the characters have scales or where all the characters have orange hair. There are multiple different kinds of copies of Dune Three. Somewhere on the number line there's a large number, a binary number, somewhere on the number line. If a prime number exists, then this number exists, okay, and decodes through the DVD codec, or, you know, the 4k codec, as a copy of Dune Two with this variation. What we do with generative AI is we train models to direct us to increase the likelihood that when we prompt them, we will land in a number on the number line, really a sequence of numbers, but I'm kind of collapsing space and time here. A number on the number line that we then take to be a meaningful digital object. Now that digital object is the interesting thing. In terms of a file, you can plug this into a robot and you can do things in the physical world with it. You can plug it into a CAD machine, or a CNC machine, and you can mill a weapon or, you know, a toy. Ultimately, I think that Gen AI is a search, a search technology. We can find a number that has components that we interpret. We bring our baggage to that number and we interpret it as this thing.

Bolchini: It's interesting the comparison with search that you made, because yesterday we were discussing the exhibit and giving a tour of the exhibit to some of the guests. And at one point of the exhibit, we showed the difference between using Google and using generative AI. ChatGPT and Google, it seems like they work like a table of content on documents that already exist, and they kind of get it for you, link it to you. And generative AI is impressive because it somehow makes that content in the moment. The content conceptually is their summary space, but it's basically concocting it in that moment. Sometimes it is very accurate. Sometimes it's not accurate, but actually very fluent. It's impressive how content made up in the moment is accurate.

Stokes: I think the search metaphor is great, because many creative people, musicians, they experience creativity as a kind of search process. Somebody will say that this song came to me, or I, you know, I discovered this piece of music. It's like it is already there somewhere and then you came across it, and it came through you.

Bolchini: Jennifer, how do you see generative AI impacting the work of people in society at large? We've heard a lot about lawyers using generative AI to search cases and find legal arguments. Of educators using this. We have seen creative artists using generative AI. How do you see this evolving in these days?

Strong: The easiest way to think about it at a societal level is that generative AI seem to come from nowhere, which is not the case, right?

It's actually older than we think. The work has been going on for decades. But about a year and a half ago, it flew onto the scene and inspired society. Suddenly, there was more interest in technology than I can ever recall, and people had something interesting to create with, to play with, to capture their imaginations. And then fairly quickly, like six months later, you had a man known as the father of deep learning, Geoffrey Hinton, quit his job at Google and come forward and say, I have real concerns this technology might actually end us, control us, take over society.

And then you had folks like Sam Altman come forward and say, The stuff I'm building at OpenAI is so powerful, it's so important, so massive, it might end us, so we have to be really, really careful. Oh and by the way, you can get your Enterprise Version of OpenAI in Aisle Five. You don't want to know what's going to happen when your competitors get hold of it, so, you know, buy now. [*audience laughter*] It was the strangest industry/society pivot to a weird marketing pitch. To me, anyway. Is industry using it? Yes, it's being used in sectors everywhere, all the places you describe. But fundamentally, 2023 was about productivity, an efficiency tool. This was in every sector everywhere, a way to save time and money. We can write emails faster, we can search faster. We can sift through stuff faster. Sure, drug discovery, that's an area where we have drugs in the pipeline now that were created with this technology, and there are other examples, but I don't think we know yet what is coming. I think 2024 is just the start of when we're going to start to see applications that aren't so broad.

Bolchini: Right now, AI is able to do a first draft of anything to a certain point, right to a certain level, at least a first draft of anything.

Strong: Yes, but we saw the film industry really step up and say, Hey, you're going to cut our pay because you're taking away the part that is most unique to us and most valued about us. You're going to give us a first draft of a movie and then tell us just to make it good. And it's never worked that way. So rather than putting the tech on us, why don't you let us, the experts, tell you what we can do with this tech to be more efficient. And I think we're going to see a lot more of that going forward.

Bolchini: Some of the worries and concerns we see in the popular media are really about this technology replacing the work that we used to do. This continuum between replacing our abilities or augmenting our abilities, and also transforming the way we do work, transforming jobs we talk a lot about, for example, prompt engineering as a new kind of job that wasn't available necessarily a few years ago, given to generative AI. John, how do you see this kind of continuum between augmenting the abilities or replacing the abilities and transforming what we do?

Stokes: Not to get all MBA, but I think that people will sort of move up the value chain. In the work that I do as a programmer with Gen AI, I find myself reading code and editing code as if this were written by a junior programmer. If I'm a writer, I may find myself reading an outline from Gen AI or reading a summary or first draft, the kind of thing that I might assign an intern to do. It can do these sorts of lower level service-type tasks very well, but then it requires me to direct it, and so it augments me. As the capabilities increase, I think it will continue to do more and more different kinds of things at a higher level of confidence. And then humans will move up, sort of get promoted to higher levels of directorial position. It *will* replace some kinds of labor. We were talking earlier in the green room about earnings call writeups. Journalists maybe spend many hours in their career listening to earnings calls for that one quote, or reading transcripts, but now you can just dump a whole transcript and a press release in there. You can press a button and you get a really nice inverse pyramid news story that hits all the highlights and pulls out some pretty good quotes.

That is a kind of work that an AI can now do that nobody in my field really wanted to do. You didn't want that gig. But then the flip side is that doing all of that kind of trains you, it makes you better. And so I think that we may have a talent pipeline problem in the future because of Gen AI, if it takes over the low level stuff. But I'll be gone. You'll be gone. That's somebody else's problem. [*audience laughter*] Not really. It's gonna be all our problem. It's worth thinking about.

Bolchini: Jennifer, what's your response to these fears and opportunities?

Strong: I agree with him about the talent pipeline. I think just because something will eventually work out where it benefits hopefully everybody — doesn't mean it starts that way. That was true of the Industrial Revolution. Going into a factory made us more efficient, but it didn't make us more human. It stripped away a lot of what made us human, and it took a very long time to get a wage that was fair, or to get more of the things that we now think about and take for granted. I think we need to be respectful to people who are fearful, because this is about cutting jobs right now. This is about savings. The extra money companies find because of AI is not being reinvested. Great analysts and thinkers have all been warning, I'd say, since probably the middle of last year: Hey, you companies, you cannot cut your way to greatness. If people are feeling fretful, it makes sense. We're in a stressful moment, and we do have a talent pipeline issue. How do you get an investigative reporter if you don't have a newsroom and you don't have that mentorship, that job, that on the job training?

By the way, these models all stand on the shoulders of human productivity of generations and generations. So if society loses access to reporters and journalism that it can trust, those models do too, and over time, what does that mean for them? And if artists can no longer afford to create the artwork that helps these models to grow and learn? I mean, there are computer scientists who predict that some of the models will eventually collapse because they're just like inbreeding and ingesting their same stuff – generative AI in, generative AI out. I don't know, I'm not a fortune teller, I'm just a journalist. So when it happens, I'll write it down.

There's so many open questions about the moment we're in and how we get from here to there, and reminding us all that we had to drive in a car before we knew we needed a seat belt. It's not like it's somebody's fault that we haven't figured everything out yet, because we haven't lived the moment yet to know what we need to do the next moment.

Bolchini: The topic of big generative AI for journalists and accuracy is a very big topic – hallucinations and understanding, what these generative AI engines really know, if in fact they know anything in the proper sense of the word. The topic of hallucination is very much on the rise. I was wondering, what is your experience with hallucination in AI work? When something is very off. There was an article that just recently came out on *Ars Technica* about Air Canada, which is being forced to pay back the ticket to a customer who was advised by a chatbot about the reimbursements policy. They were not accurate with respect to Air Canada policies. So this is one of the many, many examples we see every day of people all over society struggling with AI hallucination, and that has big, big implications.

Strong: The whole reason we started using AI was to sift through lots of data and examples and look for patterns and pattern matching, because we as humans are not fabulous at that. And so now we're putting ourselves in a position where we've come full circle, and we're having to take all this stuff and start looking through it, define the parts. As a journalist, if I'm looking through a stack of paper, I'm going to be wondering, is the math right, is this right? A friend and colleague of AI researcher Gary Marcus used AI to generate books about his life and his work. You could go hundreds of pages and be like, That's right, right, right — but he has a pet chicken in these books, and he does *not* have a pet chicken in his Manhattan apartment, to be clear. But Henrietta is very much in this stuff, buried way deep, and now it's like, entrenched in the world. Gary Marcus has a pet chicken, Henrietta, and you can't really make it go away. Was I looking for the chicken? No, I just happened to know he doesn't have a pet chicken. But for everybody else, what is the cost of the errors that slip through? AI is not a simple database, like if we decide to delete something that's not true after it's gone through this machine learning process; you can't really do that. Microsoft Research spent seven months last year trying to see if it could help a model forget something, and it couldn't figure out how.

Bolchini: How do you see the problem of hallucination in your work?

Stokes: First off, I just want to say that I think that Gary Marcus's pet chicken story is delightful, and now I want to read it. Hallucination is a feature and not a bug. For the first time, we have computers that can make things up, and they make up things that are plausible and that are interesting. And there are some cases in which this is delightful and novel, and this is not a capability that we had before. So you have to pick: Do you want the computer to invent things that are cool, or do you want the computer to just stick to what it knows? That's the first thing I would say about hallucination.

The second thing I would say about it is that, as a journalist who has been using models to do some writing and some reporting, the machine makes up things. In the way that journalists make up things, right? Insiders are saying, are, you know, right, right? The AI fixes quotes. Sometimes you get a quote from someone and GPT-4 kind of cleans it up a bit. Is that legit? If a human editor cleaned it up, it might slide. If an AI cleans it up...maybe it wouldn't slide for you. I think it's actually a bit complicated.

Strong: I will circle this back to a professor who teaches students how to litigate cases involving sexual discrimination and sexual assault, who now is associated with those words and himself appears to be accused by AI of committing these crimes, and cannot seem to extract himself from that. Truth matters.

Bolchini: The very fact that these tools can replicate what we used to do just by learning from human example, by billions and billions of text samples and images, makes us wonder: Is there anything irreducible in the human creative act, in human work? Are we being reduced to computational, efficient generators, or is there an extra dimension in the work that we do?

Stokes: I'm gonna be the contrarian here, and say, Probably not. I think I would say that if your sense of your humanity is invested in your ability to manifest, to manifest an artifact of certain quality, you are probably in trouble. In the next decade, the AIs will make really stunning and convincing visual and auditory and textual artifacts, that if you were to place them in a context and advertise them as being made by a humans or a master, people would receive it and would have some kind of artistic experience. So I think if what it is to be human is to be able to make a thing of a certain quality, then, well, you know, the jig is up.

If humanity is in our relationships, if it's in how we intend towards one another, if a text artifact isn't just a thing that I made for profit that's to be used in a certain way, if it's a thing that I mean towards *you*, that I intend towards you, and you receive it in some way, and we synchronize, like as a person to another person — then I don't think there is any danger from AI.

Strong: Except for the companies making AI girlfriends and some of the other things that extend out from there. [*audience laughter*] I don't think we know the answer to that question yet. There are other ways to answer that question, but from a nuts and bolts, write-it-down-and-improve-it one, we're human, so we're probably not the best ones to say whether or not other things are like us, and we're not very good at separating out what we know versus what we believe. Which, if you're trying to define it that way, you might need to do, but I would back us up and remind us of a time not so long ago when IBM's Big Blue beat Garry Kasparov at chess, and it caused an existential crisis, because for a very long time computer scientists had looked at chess as a measure of intelligence. It was a way to, you know, look at and decide whether a machine was about to achieve human-level intelligence. And so what did it mean? Was a singularity near? After we calmed down a moment, no, the same computer that could win at chess couldn't win at checkers yet. It also couldn't go do our laundry or make macaroni or, you know, tie some shoes. It just couldn't. I would say that right now, for this moment in generative AI, we're kind of in the same space. What does it means to live a human life and, you know, be humanity?

Bolchini: Because on the one hand, this generative AI engine cannot exist without human creativity, right? They have been created by researchers and scientists who actually marveled at these inventions. On the other hand, these tools are actually using human creative acts, you know, and ingesting all the human creativity in terms of artifacts to learn from the structure. It seems that human creativity is also at center stage to make these tools possible.

Strong: Even five years ago, we were still questioning whether a machine could be creative at all. Do we know what five years from now looks like? No, we don't.

Bolchini: Where do we go from here? You know, if you had to reflect with maybe an open question that you have in your work, as you talk to people about the future of AI and the future of us. What's the burning question you have in your mind?

Stokes: I guess my burning question is, Is OpenAI going to release something that destroys my startup? [*audience laughter*] Apart from the purely mercenary, I will just say that what I worry about is — to Jennifer's point about AI girlfriends and VR — that people might forsake human connection for a world of their own construction, chasing whatever appetites that might drive them, seemingly without any kind of consequence or check from reality, and isolate themselves. I think some people will isolate, and some people's minds will kind of bifurcate and leave the collective.

Then there are those of us that'll try and maintain real connections and relationships, and in some cases, maybe use some Gen AI to augment those. I mean, the promises for translation and for other kinds of work are tremendous. Gen AI maximizes communication bandwidth, so for people whose language skills may be awkward, who are bad at putting together linguistic constructs, can sort of get their ideas through with generative AI. So it *can* be a communication aid, but I worry about it becoming an obsession or an end in itself, a way that people escape and grow farther apart.

Bolchini: It reminds me what you're saying about the Eliza effect of the 1960s. Some early chatbots were so fluent that actually people started to believe that they were sentient beings. That these tools are very powerful but are actually at the service of a greater work, we would say, a greater mind, is actually a constructive perspective.

Strong: During the pandemic, I spent time covering people using Replica for companionship, and I will say, for one professor in particular, his companion texting him all day long was very realistic, and had been trained on him for years. From the social sciences point of view, it's like, well, this is a person who otherwise was deeply depressed and alone for a year, so how terrible is it? But on the other hand you're going, Oh my gosh, this is a very deep relationship with something that simply isn't there.

I trade in questions more than answers. The largest companies driving all this change, they are not making any money. Silicon Valley does that a lot: they lose money but have a business model for eventual profit. What is the business model? There's my question, because they will not be sustained forever off our 20 bucks a month. In a lot of situations it's really hard to make the case for these enterprise versions, which just don't differentiate enough from the free version to make it worth it. I think at one point, OpenAI was spending $700,000 a day just on power and training. At what point will there be some money in this? And what happens if there's *never* money in this? Will it just stop? What does that mean?

I think another thing I'll be watching this year will be for a shift, seeing this become more useful beyond just an efficiency tool, to see people begin to create those differentiating types of applications by sector. And I think we're going to see more of what we saw last year with the Actors Guild standing up for themselves, people in San Francisco sticking cones on self driving cars to shut them down on their tracks because they had them driving circles in their cul de sac, and they didn't feel safe with their kids or dogs. I think we're gonna see more people just saying, Okay, technology is great, but what's the purpose, and who does it serve, and why is it here?

Bolchini: I want to invite everyone to visit the exhibit on the fifth floor, on AI, work, wonder and creating. And I want to extend our thanks to our guests being here. Thank you. [*audience applause*]

Tearing Open the Sleeping Soul

A Torn Open Wound

A conversation on the war between Israel and Hamas, its worldwide impact, and any conceivable road to peace, with **Shadi Hamid**, *Washington Post columnist and editorial board member, and* **Jacob Siegel**, *senior editor at* The Tablet. *Moderated by* **Everett Price**, *foreign policy advisor.*

Introduction

There is no doubt that what started on October 7 has torn open our souls and raised many questions. Many factors have to be taken into account, and multiple points of view have to be considered if we want to address these questions without being left at the mercy of immediate reactions or prejudices. Speakers will help the audience to appreciate the complexities and nuances of this tragic situation and share how it is affecting them.

Everett Price, moderator: Good afternoon, and on behalf of the Encounter, welcome to all those joining us here at the Metropolitan Pavilion and those joining us online. I'm Everett Price, a foreign policy advisor, and I will be moderating this event. Before starting, I'd like to thank AVSI-USA for its generous support in organizing this conversation. The title for this discussion draws from the theme of the Encounter this year, and in the explanation of the theme, we find these lines: "We are ill at ease with our apathy because we are made to desire. We feel empty when we check out because we weren't meant to be checked in."

These words describe how many people around the world feel in the wake of Hamas' surprise attack on Israel on October 7 and the ensuing conflict in Gaza, which every day threatens to spread beyond. Apathy is practically inconceivable in the face of these realities because our hearts instinctively recognize that something great is at stake. The desire to organize this panel arose from the very recognition that we cannot look away; instead, we want to look deeper, painful as that may be. Indeed, a wound has been torn open, and this wound is felt first and foremost by the Israeli and Palestinian people.

On October 7, Hamas terrorists, based in the Gaza Strip, mounted a surprise attack on Israel with brazen, cold-blooded assaults primarily targeting civilians in numerous kibbutzim and a music festival, along with several security installations. These terrorists murdered approximately 1,200 people and took 240 hostages. This was the single deadliest day in Israeli history and the largest single-day loss of life for Jews since the Holocaust.

In the following weeks, Israel has mounted a widespread military campaign to end Hamas' rule over the Gaza Strip, which Hamas has controlled since 2007. This assault has claimed the lives of nearly 29,000 people, according to the Health Ministry in Gaza. Israel's military operation has faced widespread international condemnation for its toll on civilians, its impact on Gaza's 2.2 million residents, and its uncertain final objective.

But if a wound has been torn open, it suggests that the initial injury happened in the past and that efforts have been made to heal it. This injury dates back at least to the establishment of the State of Israel in 1948, which is remembered by Palestinians as the Nakba, or catastrophe, when around 700,000 Palestinians were displaced from the land that would become Israel. On the other hand, it is remembered by Israelis as their victory over the combined forces of four Arab armies that sought to squelch the dream of Israeli statehood in its infancy. The ensuing decades saw countless efforts to reconcile these two sides, to find an enduring arrangement for coexistence, but to no avail.

Today, we have invited two distinguished commentators, deeply familiar with Palestinian and Israeli points of view, to help us make sense of the facts and implications of the events we are reading about every day in the headlines. We are here to take seriously our intent to understand what is going on, why it is happening, and how we are meant to respond.

To that end, we are honored to have with us, to my left, Jacob Siegel, a contributing editor at Tablet magazine, a Jewish magazine about the world. Jacob is also the author of a forthcoming book from Henry Holt exposing the history of the war on disinformation and how it created an American censorship industrial complex. He hosts the podcast Manifesto with novelist Phil Klay.

We also have with us Shadi Hamid, a columnist and member of the editorial board at The Washington Post, and a research professor of Islamic Studies at Fuller Seminary. Previously, he was a senior fellow at the Brookings Institution. He's the author of several books, including the most recent The Problem of Democracy. He is also the co-founder of Wisdom of Crowds, a podcast, newsletter, and debate platform. Please join me in welcoming them. [*audience applause*]

So, gentlemen, thank you for being with us today, for having this conversation, and for helping us grapple with these questions. Before we dig into the substance of the conflict we're here to discuss, I want to ask a more personal question: What factors have influenced your personal approach to this conflict? What do you bring to the table when you think about it? Jacob, we can start with you.

Jacob Siegel: Thank you. I'm very glad to be here at the Encounter. I live in Israel, in central Israel, and I'm raising my two children there. So, I have a very personal stake in the conflict, and yet I'm also American, and my formative experiences were in America. I served in the U.S. Army. I was in Iraq in 2006 and 2007, and in Afghanistan in 2012. Since then, as a writer, I've spent a lot of time thinking about both the philosophy and the outcomes of the American way of war. I've developed a critique of that way of war, based on its pretenses, its self-understanding, and its actual accomplishments—or lack thereof—in the world. If I could summarize it, I'd say that the American way of war since 9/11 has been a disastrous failure.

I don't claim to be an expert on Israeli politics, and in fact, I've written only two pieces on Israeli politics in the past five years. One of them was an essay—maybe we'll talk about it later—arguing to end U.S. aid to Israel.

And prior to that, I wrote something in 2018 criticizing the militarism and bluster of Benjamin Netanyahu and the ruling faction in Israel. So, I have written a bit about Israel, but the main focus of my analysis has been the American way of war and how it's shaped the global security environment, particularly in the Middle East.

Price: Shadi?

Shadi Hamid: I guess Jacob and I are both children of the post-9/11 era. 9/11 is really one of the main reasons I decided to go into politics and policy. It happened two weeks into my freshman year of college, and ever since then, I've been thinking about U.S. foreign policy and studying it. I've also lived for many years in the Middle East. I'm not Palestinian, but I am Arab, originally Egyptian. For anyone who grows up in an Arab household, the Palestinian plight is always going to be discussed to one degree or another at the dinner table. In many ways, the plight of Palestinians is a proxy for a deeper set of issues.

When we talk about the Israeli-Palestinian conflict, what makes it so difficult and emotional is that we're not just talking about Gaza, or Palestine; we're talking about something that touches on a broader Arab sense of loss. We used to hear that we were one of the greatest civilizations the world had ever seen, but then Arabs went through one of the most precipitous declines in human history. And if you look at the Middle East now, it is pretty much an unmitigated disaster, governed by brutal dictatorships that thwart the dreams and hopes of more than 200 million people. So, when we're trying to understand why the Palestinian issue is such an emotional one, we have to consider it in this broader context of failure.

I have to be honest: I don't actually like writing much about Israel and Palestine. It's something that, for a long time, I didn't necessarily avoid, but it wasn't my favorite topic. I started at The Washington Post the week before October 7. The night of October 6, I was at a party with some friends, some of whom were journalists in D.C., and I told a journalist friend, "Oh, you know, I'm excited about this new job. No one cares about the Middle East anymore, so I'm looking forward to writing about where my heart really is, which is the role of religion in public life." The following morning, everything changed. My first five columns for The Washington

Post were on Gaza and Israel, and I feel like I've been thrust back into it, and it's been quite hard.

I find it difficult to talk about Gaza, and I've taken a break from writing about it. My last three columns haven't been about the conflict. Oddly enough, my most recent column, a couple of days ago, was about polyamory. I run the gamut of topics, I guess you could say. I'll just end by saying that this reminds me a bit of the post-9/11 era, when it felt very personal and challenging to be an Arab or a Muslim in America. I think many of us who are Arab and Muslim Americans have been hit hard by this, and we can get into why that might be the case. There's also the sense that our own government—this time, the Biden Administration—has been unquestioningly on one side and has not constrained the Israeli military operation. Many of us have had to grapple with the reality that the country we love is supporting what feels like a tragedy of nearly unprecedented proportions, at least in the context of the Israeli-Palestinian conflict, with the sheer number of Gazans being killed or displaced. It is truly unprecedented in that regard. So, that's maybe a way to introduce my thinking.

Price: Thank you for sharing that, because I think it touches on many of the themes we'll hopefully draw out in this conversation. We'll definitely get to the role of the United States and your respective views on U.S. foreign policy and its role in this conflict.

Let's start with October 7, which for many of us put this conflict back into the headlines and public awareness after some time where it seemed to be on the back burner. I'm interested in your perspectives on what happened on October 7th – and more importantly, maybe, why? Why did it happen?

Siegel: What happened was a long-planned, thoroughly rehearsed, and spectacularly successful cross-border combined arms operation by Hamas, targeting Israeli civilians. This was carried out with what we now know to be the full support of Iran, and through joint planning with Hezbollah. So, this was not Hamas acting in isolation. It wasn't Hamas simply, or even primarily, acting on behalf of the Palestinian people. This was an Iranian-backed, highly intensive military operation, the likes of which had previously been more characteristic of Hezbollah and had not been seen from Hamas before.

The operation, the praxis, the practical reality of Hamas' political ideology, was to slaughter thousands of Israeli civilians and then take hundreds back as hostages.

As to why this happened, I think it has to do with Hamas' understanding of its own position in the Middle East and its stance vis-à-vis Iran and the U.S. within a shifting global order. I believe Hamas recognized an opportunity, partly based on the U.S. security posture in the region, and partly because Iran was pushing for something to destabilize the Arab-Israeli normalization that was taking place.

Also, from a tactical and operational perspective, there was a breakdown in Israel's security architecture. The Israelis were lulled into a false sense of security regarding what Hamas was and what it wanted. We can see this, for instance, in the negotiations that preceded the October 7 attack, specifically regarding work permits for Gazan civilians to work in Israel. The number of permits had increased, reflecting a widespread belief that Hamas could be moderated through economic incentives and improvements in the quality of life.

This was a broadly shared consensus, not only in the D.C. foreign policy class but also in Israel, among both major political parties. This wasn't just a belief held by the right or the left in Israel; it was a generational consensus. Now, obviously, it looks like a generational delusion. They thought Hamas could be incentivized to act as a rational and moderate group. But clearly, Hamas was aware of this perception, manipulated it, and used it to create a false sense of security in Israel that allowed them to execute the October 7 attack.

Price: Shadi, what are your thoughts on all of that?

Hamid: Well, I agree with Jacob that it wasn't just Israelis who were lulled into complacency. The international community, and certainly the U.S., were also complacent. There's always a tendency to think that the Israeli-Palestinian conflict can be ignored or pushed to the side, and there was this sense that it was being managed. It's interesting—National Security Advisor Jake Sullivan said just eight days before October 7 that the Middle East hadn't been this quiet in two decades. It's hard to imagine the kind of self-satisfaction we had among U.S. policymakers.

The fact is, there's an Israel-Hamas war every few years, and each time we think, "Well, it passed this time, now we can move on to other things." The lesson, I think, is that the Middle East is never going to be quiet. The Israeli-Palestinian situation is never going to be quiet unless there's a real commitment to, I would say, a two-state solution.

Some of my friends and colleagues on the pro-Palestinian side (I don't love these labels, but if we have to use them) might say a one-state solution, but I don't think that's realistic. This broader conflict has been festering for decades. I think there was a big debate after October 7 about where to start the clock in discussing the tragedy. What Hamas did was horrific, and it was a surprise to most observers of the region, maybe even to some within Hamas. There's debate about who in Hamas knew about the attacks before they happened, though we don't need to get into that.

What I think is crucial here is understanding why terrorism happens. After 9/11, we realized that to prevent future attacks, we had to understand the contextual factors that lead to them—the so-called root causes. There needs to be a similar effort here. If we just start the clock on October 7, say Hamas is evil (which may be fine to say), and that Hamas needs to be destroyed, we end up with a very short-term approach. It doesn't address the broader context of the conflict. Otherwise, we'll keep returning to this cycle indefinitely.

There's also been a decades-long occupation. Gaza has been in desperate straits since 2007, with the land, air, and sea blockade, and we thought we could ignore Gaza and continue this indefinitely. But that's clearly not going to happen. I hope that this time around, there will be real efforts to make Gaza a priority—thinking about how to rebuild and reconstruct, but also moving towards a real peace process. We can't just keep ignoring the 2.2 million Gazans, who have little hope and little to look forward to.

Siegel: Can I respond to that? I have a fundamentally different understanding of Gaza's role in the Israeli-Palestinian conflict, not only regarding what led to October 7, but also how the U.S. has approached it. There's an argument I've heard that October 7 was, in some ways, a response to the marginalization of Gazans and the Palestinian plight. I don't think that's correct.

The evidence I'd present is that the marginalization occurred much more dramatically under the Trump administration, right? So, if it was the sidelining of the Palestinian plight that caused or even provided the immediate pretext for this kind of attack, we would have seen it under the Trump administration. But we didn't.

And to that point, there hasn't actually been a war between Israel and Hamas every couple of years. There was a war in 2008, then 2014, then 2021, and then 2023. So, yes, there's a risk of war every five years or so, but there was a large gap in between, and that gap occurred during the Trump administration. People on both the pro-Israeli and pro-Palestinian sides would agree that the deliberate effort of the Trump administration was to say, "We don't have to solve the Israeli-Palestinian crisis first; we can achieve Arab-Israeli normalization."

Now, the Trump administration did have its "deal of the century," so they didn't ignore the issue altogether. But the criticism from pro-Palestinian groups was that the Trump administration was deliberately sidelining the Palestinian plight. And yet, if we look at the timeline, when do these wars flare up? It's not quite every few years. There's a large gap in the middle, and that gap corresponds to the period when, according to the pro-Palestinian argument, marginalization was the most intense.

When Biden came into office, his day-one decision was to restart funding to UNRWA, for instance, which Trump had cut off, and to refocus attention on the Palestinian plight and the Israeli-Palestinian conflict, returning it to the preeminence it had lost. So, if we're not just looking at this in theoretical terms but studying the correlation between policies and events, it actually shows something different. It paints a different picture.

Hamid: I know you probably want to move on, Everett, but I would just take issue with the idea that the Biden administration prioritized the Palestinian plight. There was nothing of the sort. Biden's policy has essentially doubled down on Trump's. He has taken the Abraham Accords—which, as you said, were designed around sidelining the Palestinians—and continued to ignore them. That has been central to Biden's approach.

I'd go further and say Biden has been, to not mince words, terrible when it comes to anything related to the Palestinians. The way he talks about Palestinians is incredibly disrespectful. There was a very memorable moment that went viral a few weeks after October 7, when a reporter asked Biden about the civilian death toll, and he just dismissively said, "Well, we can't even trust the numbers." Sure, there can be legitimate debate about exactly how many have been killed, but when 7,000 or 8,000 people have died, the difference of a thousand more or less shouldn't be the main issue.

The heart of the question was that people wanted Biden to express basic sympathy for the loss of Palestinian lives, but he wasn't able to do that. Time and time again, reporters have asked senior U.S. officials to simply show that they see Palestinians as human beings deserving of dignity and equal worth. And that's what really hurts a lot of us.

I'm not someone who would argue that Israel doesn't have a right to defend itself. Of course, Israel does. But the complete lack of balance in how Biden talks about both sides is really hard to understand. Obama, for instance, could speak with empathy toward both Palestinians and Israelis. He could speak to the historical narratives on both sides. And while both-sidesism is often maligned—people say you must pick one side or the other—I want my president to acknowledge what Palestinians are going through.

Instead, we hear statements like, "War is tragic," which is what John Kirby, a White House spokesperson, said in another viral moment: "War is tragic. Lives are lost. This is what happens." That kind of insensitivity has been at the heart of the Biden administration's approach.

This is why, and this may be a bigger issue, so many Arab and Muslim Americans are saying they might not vote for Biden later this year if his policy doesn't change. Voting is an act of conscience, and it's becoming difficult for a lot of Arab Americans to support a president who seems not to care on a fundamental level.

Price: This is an interesting disagreement because you're both looking at the same picture but seeing very different takeaways—either that Biden is doing too little, or he's doing way too much. I definitely want to dig more into that. You've also raised the issue of the root causes and what this conflict is really about. Jacob, you mentioned the period of conflict and then the period where there was no conflict, which raises the question for me: Is there a sustainable status quo for the Israeli-Palestinian conflict? Is there a coexistence—either now or in the future—that could allow both sides to live in peace?

I welcome your thoughts on this framing. It seems like there are two different communities with aspirations that have found those aspirations in conflict. One way to characterize this might be Israel's desire to live in peace on the one hand, and on the other, the Palestinians' desire for self-determination and statehood, similar to how Israel achieved statehood in the first half of the 20th century. What do you make of that characterization? And I guess this also brings up the question: Do we need a two-state solution? Is there a sustainable coexistence possible between the two?

Siegel: I don't know, and I don't think anybody knows. I certainly don't presume to have an answer to that. Time will tell. That doesn't mean it's not a worthy goal. Palestinian self-determination and Palestinian statehood are important, just as Jewish self-determination and Jewish sovereignty are important, but they're not the same thing. Statehood is a vehicle for sovereignty and self-determination, but historically, that hasn't always been the case. There are other models of sovereignty and self-determination.

So, I simply don't know what the formula for peaceful, long-term coexistence is, and I don't assume that just because it's a desirable or moral outcome, it's necessarily achievable. If a solution does exist, it will likely come from Israelis and Palestinians, perhaps with guidance from regional powers. But my faith in technocrats in Washington figuring this out is nil. I look at other cases—Afghanistan, Ukraine, COVID policy—and see where the technocratic consensus has not only been mistaken but disastrous. So, I have no desire to award power to think tanks in Washington to figure this out.

That's not to say there isn't a role for outside powers, especially regional ones, who are more invested in the realities of the conflict and may have more credibility. But just because the two-state solution is a popular political formula, palatable to people across the board, doesn't mean it can be grafted onto the conflict and work simply because people want it to. There has to be real buy-in from the people involved.

The last thing I'd say is about the two-state solution model. I'm not opposed to a two-state solution, but there's a difference between "a" two-state solution and "the" two-state solution, which has become the default formula among foreign policy elites in Washington and Brussels. Given how much has already been invested in that formula over the decades, I don't see any reason to believe that now, just because there's been a brutal massacre in Israel followed by a brutal war in Gaza, that this is the moment it's going to work—just because the Biden administration decides it wants it to.

Hamid: I think, in the short term, the priority should be mitigating civilian harm. There's a real risk now that Israel will launch a major offensive into Rafah, which would be devastating. It's worth reminding people of the scale of the disaster so far: More than 80% of the Gazan population has been displaced, and around 28,000 people have been killed. If we assume that about a third of them are combatants—which is based on past conflicts and might be a conservative estimate—then around two-thirds are civilians. We're talking about a massive number of civilians killed.

I recently compared this with the number of civilians directly killed by U.S. military operations in Iraq from 2003 to 2011. According to Iraq Body Count, the number was about 14,000. After just about 100 days of the Israel-Gaza war, the number of civilians killed had already exceeded that, reaching around 16,000 of a total 24,000. The scale is really shocking.

This raises the question of whether the U.S. can do more to pressure Israel. Again, I'm not saying Israel doesn't have the right to defend itself, but there has to be a serious commitment to civilian protection, and we haven't seen that when it comes to Israeli military operations. That's step one.

In the medium to long term, I don't think there's another option besides a two-state solution—unless we want to talk about a binational state, which would be even worse for Israelis. That would go against the idea that Jews have a right to self-determination and that Israel has a right to exist as a Jewish state. A binational state would be correcting one injustice with another. Why would Israeli Jews want to be subsumed into a binational

Arab-Jewish state where they could eventually become a minority in their own land? That seems like an unjust solution.

The other alternatives are annexation or indefinite military occupation, which I hope we can avoid. So, by process of elimination, the only realistic option is a Palestinian state in Gaza, the West Bank, and East Jerusalem as its capital, living side by side with Israel.

The only way that can happen is if the U.S.—Israel's primary military patron—puts real pressure on Israel. Israel depends on the U.S. to maintain one of the region's strongest, most technologically advanced militaries. I understand that Israelis are in retribution mode right now and may not be in the mood to consider Palestinian civilian lives. But as Americans, we don't have to go along with that. We can be critical of our friends and say to Israel: "This might be okay with you, but it's not okay with us, because our military hardware and assistance are implicated in this civilian tragedy."

That's where the U.S. has leverage, and for all of Washington's faults, I don't see who else is going to put pressure on Israel. The U.S. is really the only party that has the legitimacy and leverage with Israel going forward.

Price: Yeah, I guess the big question on a lot of people's minds right now is, okay, we're several months, I guess, into this Israeli operation in the Gaza Strip. What is the end state envisioned by the Israelis who are creating the strategy and mounting the offensive in Gaza? As you said, it doesn't necessarily have to be a two-state solution. The Prime Minister of Israel, Benjamin Netanyahu, has said he rejects the idea of a two-state solution. So has there been an articulated end game for what the Israeli military is doing in Gaza right now? What do you see as the future of the people of Gaza in light of what's happening?

Siegel: I have not seen an articulated political endgame coming formally from the Prime Minister's Office in Israel, which I think is a real problem and a significant one that has gotten a lot of criticism and deserves it. The failure to enunciate an endgame—sometimes portrayed by statesmen as strategic ambiguity—means, in a democratic society, they don't even have to formulate it for themselves. So my faith in Netanyahu and his cabinet having some brilliant endgame that they're keeping private is very low, perhaps nonexistent. However, there is a very clear military strategy and military end state. Netanyahu has laid it out, and it has three components: destroy Hamas, demilitarize Gaza, and de-radicalize Gaza.

I think the first two components—destroying Hamas and demilitarizing Gaza—are, practically speaking, achievable goals that relate to a clearly defined end state. Strategically, they match ends to means in a way that is legible and achievable. The last part, however—de-radicalizing Gaza—is a problem for me. I don't think it's Israel's responsibility, nor is it necessarily within its capacity, to ideologically or culturally transform Gaza's society. Exactly this kind of thinking underpinned the catastrophic U.S. military adventurism in the Middle East.

Shadi made a comparison to Iraq, but I think that's the wrong comparison. For one thing, Iraq was a total strategic failure for the United States. It didn't make Americans safer, and the strategic legacy of the Iraq War was to empower Iran and turn it into a regional hegemon. That's what the U.S. accomplished in Iraq, after a decade and thousands of soldiers killed, and I think many more Iraqis than even the numbers you mentioned.

The Iraq model—the so-called population-centric or counterinsurgency model of warfare, where the U.S. launched a war of choice to transform Iraqi society and bring democracy to the Middle East—was an imperial war. That's not what Israel is fighting in Gaza. It's not an imperial war, and it's not a war of choice. It's a war that was brought to Israel on its own doorstep. The appropriate analogy, in my opinion, would be the campaign in Mosul. In Mosul, ISIS had embedded itself within a civilian population roughly the same size as Gaza—around two million people—but the ISIS force was far smaller, about 3,000 fighters compared to something like 30,000 Hamas fighters in Gaza. The ISIS fighters in Mosul also had far less advanced weaponry.

The campaign to liberate Mosul, which the United States led, destroyed about 60% of the city and killed somewhere between 10,000 to 30,000 civilians. These numbers may be new or surprising to some people because there wasn't the same fanatical global obsession with the horrific civilian toll in Mosul as there is with Gaza. A nine-month operation to liberate Mosul had similarities to what's happening in Gaza, in terms of scale of destruction and intensive bombing. It led to the liberation of Mosul from

ISIS, something most people supported, though it came at a huge cost to civilians.

The major difference is that in Mosul, about half the civilian population left before the joint U.S.-Iraqi campaign. In Gaza, the international consensus seems to be that no Gazans should be able to leave. Egypt, for its own reasons—political, ideological, and security considerations—didn't want to allow Palestinians into the Sinai. There's a general consensus that allowing civilians to leave, which has been the norm in other modern wars, especially in urban campaigns, is considered ethnic cleansing here.

Hamid: Well, yes, I mean, that's what happened before, during the Nakba. That is key to the Palestinian narrative. In 1948, Palestinians left their homes and weren't allowed to come back. That's the defining moment in the Palestinian national memory. There's no guarantee that if Gazans left and were stuck in tents in Egypt, they'd ever be allowed to return. And why would they want to live under a brutal dictatorship in Egypt, which doesn't care about them, instead of staying in their homeland? Many on the far-right in Israel's ruling coalition openly and explicitly support ethnic cleansing, and they are part of the government right now.

I would never want to encourage Palestinians to leave when there are no guarantees they could return, and, honestly, what would they even return to? Gaza is being destroyed. The whole northern part is basically destroyed. Now there's a risk that Rafah, the one place Palestinians were told was safe, will come under bombardment. Nowhere is truly safe, and there's no guarantee Gazans will have anywhere to return to.

Price: I want to touch on the internal dynamics because what's playing out internationally reflects what's happening domestically in these societies. We've already talked a bit about Israeli politics, but there has been a shift over time. Early in Israel's history, the left-wing parties dominated, and the right didn't win an election until 1977. Since then, the ruling coalitions have moved further to the right, with a larger role for conservative and ultra-Orthodox parties. Does that resonate with you? What accounts for these evolutions, and what does this mean for how Israeli society views the conflict and the neighborhood they live in?

Siegel: The evolution happens in phases. There was a post-1967 birth and growth of religious Zionism, related to the idea of returning to Judea and Samaria as the home of Judaism. This political religious Zionism had always been latent in Zionism but hadn't been as politically salient. Then there's the legacy of the failure of the Oslo Accords and the land-for-peace framework. The Israeli left failed to deliver on its promises, which led to a collapse of imagination on the right. The political right in Israel has risen, but its failure is imagining that it could keep the Palestinian issue on hold, build up the country's security, remake Israel as a startup nation, and that would be enough. I wrote in 2018 criticizing the hollowness of the post-Oslo political right. I agree with their assessment that Oslo was a failure, but that doesn't mean you stop working toward a solution that provides for the aspirations of both peoples.

The rise of the Israeli right has included people who have made despicable statements, some of which are tantamount to calls for ethnic cleansing. Some of that has been distorted in the press. For instance, Yoav Gallant, the Israeli Defense Minister, was misquoted as referring to Palestinians as animals when he was actually referring to Hamas.

Price: And Shadi, similarly, in the Palestinian territories, there's been this division between Fatah in the West Bank and Hamas in Gaza. The hope was that these factions would reconcile, but Israel has complained that they don't have a partner for peace because the Palestinians are divided. Has October 7 changed that? Do the people of Gaza hold Hamas accountable for what's happened since the attack?

Hamid: Well, there was a partner for peace for a while. As flawed as the Palestinian Authority and President Abbas were, they were more moderate than Hamas and committed to the Oslo framework. Netanyahu sidelined Abbas for years, and no progress has been made since 2013. The refrain that there's no partner for peace is self-serving and has been used to justify not doing anything in good faith to move toward peace.

At the end of the day, though, this might be an irreconcilable situation. Israelis and Palestinians currently hate each other at a fundamental level, and you can see this reflected in public opinion polls. There's been a process of dehumanization on both sides, and these memories will be seared into the consciousness of both peoples for a long time.

Price: I want to close by discussing the role of the United States. Jacob, you wrote an article in July titled "End U.S. Aid to Israel," advocating for greater Israeli autonomy in deciding its policies. Shadi, on the other hand, you've emphasized how U.S. leverage is important in advancing moral foreign policy. Should U.S. foreign policy pursue moral ends?

Siegel: U.S. policy should try to pursue ends that serve the interests of the U.S. And if the U.S. is a moral agent, those will be moral ends. This is the classical framework of U.S. foreign policy, as enunciated by John Quincy Adams: go not in search of monsters, don't attempt moral crusades throughout the world, perfect the union here, build the city on the hill. And if you build the city on the hill here, then in protecting the interests of the United States, you will be serving the cause of freedom.

Now, I think an eloquent case can be made, and I think Shadi made this, for why Palestinian, Arab, or Muslim Americans might have felt not fully seen or fully recognized. I think the Biden administration has actually tried to do more in this regard than other administrations might have. But it certainly doesn't fall on deaf ears—I can understand that argument. However, to me, what I want from the White House is not to recognize anyone or to see anyone's humanity; I want the White House to pursue policies that reduce war and violence in the world. I want there to be less killing and less warfare. And what we've seen over the last 20 years is that the more grandiose visions of a moral U.S. foreign policy have produced more killing, more wars, more destabilization. If the U.S. could narrow what it is trying to accomplish and focus on protecting its own peace, I think both the U.S. and the world would be better off.

In the Middle East specifically, I think there's a very widespread misconception of what the U.S. relationship to the actors in the Middle East is—a testament to the success of the messaging campaigns and the way that communications have overtaken reality, the image overtaking reality. There's this popular idea that the U.S. and Israel have a special relationship, and it's the U.S. and Israel with this really firm alliance against the rest of the Middle East. It's not true. That's not the actual U.S. relationship to Israel or to the greater Middle East, for that matter. The power of the Israel lobby in the U.S. has been declining for the past two decades. Obama would never have been able to—well, he didn't pass the Iran deal through Congress, but the success of the Iran deal, which was put through at the executive level despite congressional opposition, is a sign of how weak the pro-Israel forces in the U.S. have become.

The actual nature of the U.S. relationship to the Middle East is one of managing client states. Israel is a client state, Iran is a client state, Egypt is a client state. It's an imperial policy. This is nothing new—it's how empires have conducted their foreign policy for millennia. The real problem is not the morality or lack of morality; it's that the U.S. should not be pursuing an imperial foreign policy of balancing client states.

Just the last thing I would say is that incredible statement by Jake Sullivan, I believe eight days before October 7, in which he said that the Middle East is quieter than it has been in decades. The other thing Sullivan said in that speech was he laid out precisely the kind of clientelist imperial strategy I just described. He said the U.S. was integrating the region, depressurizing the region by integrating adversaries. In other words, like, "Yeah, they think they have their differences—Israel, Iran, Hezbollah, Hamas—but really, we can integrate all of them into our security architecture." It's been a total failure.

Hamid: I think there's some overlap between Jacob and me. I agree that one of America's goals should be to reduce harm, to reduce killing, but I believe that can be done by constraining the Netanyahu government in its current military operations. That is where there is a tremendous loss of life, and I think that's a place where we can use our leverage.

But more broadly, I'm a bit more of a moralist than Jacob is when it comes to U.S. foreign policy, and that's what makes this current moment very difficult for me. I very much believe in the American idea, and in the idea that America should express its values abroad. I've been very critical that we haven't done that in the Middle East. I mean, after the Cold War, we got better at supporting democratic transitions in Latin America, East Asia, and parts of Africa, after supporting right-wing dictators during the Cold War. The one region where we didn't support democracy was the Middle East, and to this day, we support these autocratic client states to the tune of billions of dollars, helping to prop them up and undermining democracy in the region.

It's a longer story as to why we do that. My preference, and what I've advocated for many years now, is that we should use our aid relationships with these client states—like Egypt, like Saudi Arabia—and put pressure on them to open up their societies and eventually move in a more democratic direction. Okay, for morality, but also for our interests. As a fundamental outlook, I would argue that autocratic regimes are inherently unstable because they go against what we know about human nature: that at some basic level, people want to have some jurisdiction over their own affairs. They want to be able to express themselves publicly. They want to have the chance to criticize their leaders when their leaders go astray, and autocratic regimes suppress the human spirit in a way that, I would argue, is contradictory to Christian, Muslim, and Jewish conceptions of the worth of the human individual.

So, there's a broader argument there that I think is really important and dear to me. And it hurts me that the U.S. has not been able to live up to its own stated moral commitments in the Middle East in a way that is just very blatant. My hope is that one day that can change. I'm not holding my breath, but I suppose hope springs eternal.

Price: I really appreciate that. Thank you so much, both of you, for joining us for this conversation. [*audience applause*]

STILL AWAKE!

*A presentation on this year's Encounter theme, accompanied by Msgr. Lorenzo Albacete's clarity, prescience, and wit, with greetings by **Cardinal Seán O'Malley**, Archbishop of Boston, and a conversation with **Jakub Grygiel**, professor of politics, Catholic University of America, **Fr. Ryan Mann**, pastor of St. Basil the Great Parish, Cleveland. Moderated by **Stephen Sanchez**, president of the Albacete Forum.*

Introduction

Msgr. Lorenzo Albacete's contribution to the birth and development of the Encounter has been invaluable. On the occasion of the 10th anniversary of his death, and in light of this year's Encounter theme, speakers will discuss Msgr. Albacete's original contribution to the intellectual and spiritual life of the American Catholic Church and society at large.

Stephen Sanchez, moderator: Good afternoon. Today, on behalf of the Albacete Forum, we have invited three of Lorenzo's friends to share with us not only their friendship with Lorenzo, and therefore invite you into that friendship, but also to give us a glimpse into a man whose personality and genius many of us know. And for those of you who don't, you'll have the chance to discover him. To my left is Cardinal Seán O'Malley, the Archbishop of Boston, who has known Lorenzo for as long as Lorenzo has known anything, really. Jakob Griego, who met Lorenzo as a young kid when his father was a professor at the John Paul II Institute in Rome, will tell you that he became Lorenzo's driver. And Father Ryan, a man who never knew Lorenzo in life, but who, like many of you, met him through YouTube, New York Encounter talks, and various other moments where not only the profound but also the hilarity ensued. Father Ryan is a priest in the Diocese of Cleveland, and Jakob is a professor of political science at Catholic University of America. Please welcome them with me. [*audience applause*]

Cardinal Seán O'Malley: Good afternoon, everyone. It's a great joy to be with you today and to talk about Father Lorenzo. There used to be a column in Reader's Digest called "The Most Unforgettable Person I Ever Met." I'm sure Lorenzo was a candidate for that category in many people's lives, and certainly in my own. It was my privilege to meet Lorenzo about 55 years ago. I was a young Capuchin friar, studying at Catholic University, living at the Capuchin monastery on Harewood Road. In those days, Lorenzo was working at NASA or involved in his scientific pursuits—it was before he went to the seminary. It was my joy to see him enter the seminary, to preach at his first Mass, and later to preach at his funeral Mass. For me, Lorenzo was one of the most extraordinary priests I've ever met. He truly embodied the joy of the Gospel.

Today's title for this conference, *Still Awake!*, is very fitting. I see the nuncio here, who was in Cuba. I often said that being the apostolic administrator of the seminaries in Cuba was an Alice in Wonderland-type experience. The day I arrived, the rector of the seminary told me, "Bishop, we just discovered that one of the seminarians was an infiltrator from the police." I said, "What?" He replied, "Oh yes, and we're so shocked because he was so pious, studious, and punctual." I said, "Well, that should've given it away!" [*audience laughter*]

During my visitations in Cuba, I often stayed at the nunciature. One time, the nuncio told me that Fidel Castro had come at two o'clock in the morning, rang the bell, and asked to speak with the nuns. They woke the nuns up, and Fidel said, "Sisters, I want you to prepare me a meal. I know you won't poison me." Well, like Fidel Castro, Lorenzo would often wake me up in the middle of the night—but precisely to "poison" me! He would take me to fast food places. I remember once going to IHOP at about two o'clock in the morning. Lorenzo knew everyone, and he introduced me to all these people. One was a waitress who told us, "I'm a volunteer waitress on the night shift because I'm hoping to be discovered by a Hollywood talent scout." Lorenzo always knew the most interesting people. He was always "still awake" at any time, as he used to say, *La noche está en pañales*—"The night is in diapers."

We often spoke late into the night, reading the same books, particularly Latin American literature—García Márquez, Isabel Allende—and discussing passages from those works. But with Lorenzo, you knew you could call him at any time, and he would do the same. Erasmus once described Thomas More as "born for friendship." That's a good description of Lorenzo Albacete. He was born for friendship. As the Spanish say, *tenía don de gente*—he had a gift with people. He knew everyone.

Recently, I shared with my priests in Boston what happened to me during my first Holy Week as a priest. In the seminary, you look forward to Holy Week, imagining what it will be like. But I never imagined it would be like it was. I was working with the Hispanic community at St. Matthew's Cathedral in Washington, DC. In those days, they had The Tre Ore, the three hours of prayer from 12 to 3 p.m. in English, followed by Spanish services. I was supposed to help give out communion, but when I arrived, I found the cathedral in chaos. There were two groups: the Washington Lay Association and another group called the Sons of Thunder. The Sons of Thunder, wearing red berets with rosaries around their necks, were passing out flyers, and fistfights broke out. A woman stood in the back of the church shouting, "Cardinal O'Boyle, get out here like a man and face us!" Meanwhile, the Sons of Thunder lifted the leader of the Lay Association and carried him down the aisle of St. Matthew's Cathedral. I thought, if they make it to the steps, they'll kill him. Monsignor Kuhn got there just in time to stop them. As people rushed out, screaming and yelling, television cameras were outside. An elderly woman with a mantilla and a little prayer book tried to cover the camera lens so no one could see how badly Catholics behaved on the holiest day of the year.

The reason I bring this up is because Lorenzo was dear friends with people in both the Lay Association and the Sons of Thunder. He was incredible. Pope Francis talks so much about synodality today—I wish

Lorenzo were alive because he could embody that synodality. He could speak to everyone, and he was the least threatening person you could imagine. I always say that many of the rough patches we experienced after Vatican II, in the implementation of its teachings, could have been smoothed over by someone like Lorenzo. He was a man who knew how to listen and who never judged anyone. I remember reading an article about Olaf Scholz, the Chancellor of Germany, who said, "We are never offended, and we are never hysterical." That's a good description of Lorenzo. He was never offended, never hysterical. He was always listening, always searching for the truth with love.

When Lorenzo was installed as president of the Catholic University of Puerto Rico, I was next to him on stage. He was wearing the academic robes of the university, which is dedicated to Our Lady. They were powder blue with deep blue stripes on the sleeves, and he wore a black velvet bonnet with a gold tassel, holding a ceremonial staff. He turned to me and said, "You know, Seán, if this doesn't work out, I can always get a job working with Walter Mercado." Walter Mercado was a flamboyant Hispanic psychic with extravagant wigs, jewelry, and makeup—he would make Liberace seem subdued.

Lorenzo's life was full of twists and frustrations, but I always say God had other plans for him. His life was marked by profound faith, tested by pain and loss. His beautiful work The Cry of the Heart gives insight into how deeply he understood the cross. Like the rich young man in the Gospel, Lorenzo asked the right questions and sought the right answers, but unlike the young man who went away sad, Lorenzo knew how much the Lord loved him. This knowledge liberated him and allowed him to live passionately for the church, his family, and the Communion and Liberation movement, which became his spiritual home.

For all of us who knew and loved him, we are certain that Lorenzo is still awake. God bless you. [*audience applause*]

Sanchez: Thank you, Your Eminence. Jakub?

Jakub Grygiel: Thank you. Well, between a cardinal, His Eminence, and Fr. Ryan, who, it turns out, is trained as an improv comedian, you get me, a professor of international relations.

I have two points I want to offer. The first one is about Fr. Lorenzo. As His Eminence said, he was really a man with an infinite desire for and ability to create friendships with love. I wouldn't be here—literally—even here physically, if it hadn't been for him. I came to the US, to some degree, because of him. I've known him since I was a teenager in Rome. On my first trip to the US, he found me my first job, which I assume—since there's a statute of limitations—was probably illegal. I mean, he was from Puerto Rico, no offense, but he found me a job. Where do you think the job was? A pen store. The man was a fountain pen fanatic. So, he got me a job, and I didn't speak a word of English. And there I was, selling fountain pens in downtown DC. I've seen priests and people kneel in front of altars in church. I had never seen a priest kneel at the entry of a fountain pen store.

So, you know, here I am, a teenager who grew up in the shadow of the Vatican, working illegally at a pen store, and a priest kneels there. Fr. Lorenzo helped me with my college applications—something I'm now going through with my own kids. He picked me up at then-National Airport (now Reagan Airport) when I came for my freshman year, and he even moved me into my dorm at Georgetown. Before you say, "How cute," keep in mind, he walked up to the seventh floor of Harbin Hall—and for those familiar with Georgetown, he wasn't exactly the fittest guy on the planet. He swore very colorfully, saying that after all, he was a priest, and he shouldn't be helping kids move into college. You can imagine the parents, already nervous, wondering, "What is this place?"

One last silly story: I didn't have a pillow cover, and he gave me one of his—a used one with a cigarette burn on it—which said something like, "U.S. Olympic Sleep Team." It didn't quite match the title, but I think my wife threw it away, unfortunately, because it felt like a relic to me.

On a more serious note, I am actually married because of him. He celebrated our wedding, he blessed our marriage. And you know, when I think of Fr. Lorenzo, I remember what happened during the vows. He was leading me through them, and at one point, I was looking at him while repeating after him, "I, Jakub, take you as my lawful wedded wife." Suddenly, he stopped and said, "Stop! Stop looking at me! Look at your wife! I get nervous when men look at me while professing their marriage vows!" My voice started trembling at that point. How often do you see a dramatic interruption at a wedding? That was him.

But seriously, let me share a couple of paragraphs from his homily at our wedding. Don't worry, not the whole thing, just a few parts.

"The love that unites a man and a woman in marriage is the sign of a great mystery. This mystery is engraved in the very structure of our humanity. It is experienced as an unquenchable desire of the human heart. It is a desire that aims at eternity. Indeed, the very word 'desire' has its Latin root in a reference to the stars. Think of what is called a 'starry sky' or 'desiderium.' The stars are symbols of infinity. Love always aims at infinity and a limitless forever. Love is a desire that reveals the human being to be made for infinity, capable of the eternal. This capacity, engraved in our humanity, in our flesh—weak, limited, and mortal as it is—points to the mystery searched by all religious traditions, uniting us all, regardless of differences. Love is the sign and expression of this capacity, the need for God."

Then he addressed me and my wife, but specifically me. He said:

"Therefore, Jakub, you must recognize your love for Priya (my wife) as a path and vocation to be for her a sign of Christ's love. You come to this vocation gifted with the incomparable example of your parents, the prophetic history of your people, and the experience of having grown up so close to the man to whom the faith and unity of the Church has been entrusted. Above all, you come to it with the grace of your baptism, constantly sustained and nourished by the Eucharistic offering of your love for her, just as you have done today. May your wife and children discover in your love, as husband and father, a sign of the grace through which Christ reaches out to them."

There was really nothing more real and simpler for him, and at the same time, more full of mystery, than love and friendship. He lived for love and friendship, and called all of us to do the same. Everything else for him was secondary, including, in many ways, his health. You know, he would take us to a fried chicken place while smoking cigarettes—so you can imagine what that was like—but love and friendship were absolutely essential for him.

Now, my second point, and I actually have a photo that conveys this. If it can be put up — yes, there it is. Swim trunks, right? [*audience awwwws*]

This brings me to my second point: suffering.

For those of you who are younger, we used to have answering machines in dorms and apartments. Fr. Lorenzo would often call me and leave voicemails screaming "Let it fester!" My roommates would come in, press play, and there'd be this guy yelling on the answering machine. In the picture, you see the words "Vive le festin" ("Let it fester") written in the background. We may have written it ourselves, I can't remember. You have eternity, infinity, mystery—all of that in the picture. But all of it was always linked with suffering for him. He thought more deeply about suffering than anyone I've ever known, and he lived it.

By the way, he did not mention this in our wedding homily. But in so many conversations, he repeated a very simple idea: it is human to suffer. In fact, to be human, you have to accept suffering. Some of it is physical, but much of it is not, and all of it, for him, always pointed to love.

One of the greatest formative experiences I had with him was in the '90s, when I was living in DC. I would see him almost every week. But before we did anything else, we had to visit the Little Sisters of the Poor, where his mother lived—she had Alzheimer's. Nothing else mattered to him. He had to put her to bed, say her evening prayers, and sing a Spanish lullaby to her. Only then, no matter how long it took, could we go to IHOP or grab fried chicken. His love for her was enormous, and often puzzling to others. Even if you were His Eminence, you had to wait for him. He wouldn't sacrifice that expression of love for anyone or anything else.

Three thoughts on suffering, to close. These are things I learned from him. First, suffering is the source of the great questions that make us human. St. Augustine, after the death of his best friend, wrote that he became "a great question to himself." Without suffering, we cannot fully understand who we are. Suffering is a cry for infinity and eternity.

Second, there are really bad answers to suffering. I remember when someone young, my age, died in the '90s. People said the usual things: "Find closure," "Find peace." Fr. Lorenzo got mad. He would say, "That's bullshit. I don't want closure. I don't want peace. I want that person back, in flesh and bones." Suffering is unavoidable, and don't try to offer easy answers.

Finally, there is no solution to suffering. He was clear about this. There is no grand theory of suffering. Sure, some suffering can be explained—if you bang your knee, you know why. But that doesn't solve the problem of suffering. What you do is embrace the person who is crying, not give them a theory. And this is true for all types of suffering. If you believe there is a solution, you end up wanting to eliminate the suffering—and maybe even the sufferer. Euthanasia, he would say, is one such modern "solution." But it's not what we are meant to do. The only real response to suffering is love—to suffer with the person and simply be with them.

And in that sense, Fr. Lorenzo was a great man of friendship. That's what the picture shows. We weren't suffering in that moment, but we were together as friends. For him, everything—eternity, infinity, suffering, and friendship—was one big, interconnected package.

So, I'll end on that.

Fr. Ryan Mann: Well, as was said, I'm Father Ryan Mann from Cleveland—Cleveland, Ohio. Much like Nazareth, great things come out of Cleveland. To build on what we just heard: for me, the break between those three and myself is that I never met him. So if some of you haven't met Albacete, I'm the same way. You're probably thinking, "What are you going to share if you didn't meet the guy?"

I was ordained in May of 2014, and then in October, Monsignor died. That afternoon, I had a great first assignment. It was for priests, and my Irish pastor told great stories. After dinner, I went up to my office and was looking at some Catholic blog or something, and it said, "Prominent Monsignor dies." In my diocese, a previous bishop had stopped naming Monsignors, so I was like, "There are still Monsignors?" And then I thought, "What's a prominent one?" So I clicked, and sure enough, it was Albacete.

That night began a long journey for me. I read blog after blog and commentary. I think there was a website called GodSpy—is that something? I'm not in CL, sorry, I'm an imposter. But there was a website, and he had a lot of articles there. I just binged on them. It was remarkable because I'm not what you would call academic, so the idea of spending a night reading would surprise most of my friends. But what I found in reading his work was that something resonated deeply with me. I had found someone who thought more deeply about questions I held but had never voiced. He articulated things in a way that was life-giving—a way where I felt like I could express and speak the mystery. I could speak Jesus, I could speak the Church into people's lives in a way that was a big "yes" to everything good in their lives. It wasn't, "Hey, if you do these things, maybe then we'll welcome you." That really resonated with me.

One of the things that stood out most was his childlike candidness. He was so candid. Those of you who have little kids or are around them all the time know they're very honest. I have several families I'm close to, and the little ones always climb all over me when I'm at their house. They like to run their fingers on the back of my balding head and say, "You're losing your hair." And I tell them they're grounded. But the point is, kids are very straightforward—and so was Lorenzo. He had no problem saying what everyone was feeling but no one had the courage to say.

One of his interviews was after 9/11, and it seems fitting to tell this while we're in New York. He was being interviewed, I believe on *Nightline* or something like that. They were pressuring him to say, "Okay, you're a Catholic Monsignor, what did you see when the towers were falling? What were you experiencing?" You could tell the unspoken question was, "Give us some spiritual insight we can all hold onto." And he responded, "I saw death. Human death. I've seen death in many ways, but this one made me stop. I could not move past it. I saw death." The interviewer, trying to press for some moment of hope or consolation, asked, "Well, does your faith help you?" And he said, "No." And then he added, "A thousand times, no."

When I read that, I was hooked. Finally! See, after high school, I was a professional jazz musician, and then I did Second City improv comedy. It was from those experiences that I really sensed my calling. But my calling was not a denial of the enjoyment I had in comedy clubs or jazz clubs. There was no sense — though I wouldn't have had the consciousness or articulation until years later after encountering his writings — that I needed to give any of that up to follow Christ.

What Pope Benedict said, "Christ takes nothing away that makes life beautiful, meaningful, and good," really resonated with me. All the friendships I had in the jazz world — I'm not going to say they're going to be canonized; they were jazz musicians. Everything you imagine was happening with them, right? But they were friends. They cared about me, we shared meals and stories, and I'm just old enough to say, also, CDs! We shared a lot of things together. And in the comedy world, it was the same thing. But I never felt like I had to deny any of that to follow Christ.

When I began to feel the tug to enter the seminary, it felt like a natural progression of the beauty and goodness I had already experienced. Albacete wrestled with the same things, and thank God he did, because I would never have known that they could go together. In his early years, as the Cardinal said, he was into science. He was a physicist. One day, one of his science buddies asked him, "How do you, as a scientist who believes in the laws of science five days a week, believe on Sunday that a man rose from the dead and you can talk to him and encounter him? Either you live two lives or you're crazy." Albacete said, "Coming from Puerto Rico, where even the coconuts are Catholic, I never confronted these questions." But he became obsessed with this encounter, and he'll say years later that it was those very questions that led him to the priesthood.

There's a great story about a Stations of the Cross in New York. If you didn't know him—I never met him—just stick around, and people will tell you stories. He was outside smoking a cigarette, which was his pre-spiritual practice. A lady came up to him and asked, "Are you protesting something?" And he said, "Yes." She asked, "What are you protesting?" He said, "Dualism." She walked away, and he shouted after her, "It will get you! Come back!" Like any great stand-up comedian, it was funny because it orbited around the truth.

For Albacete, he really meant it. We're not separating our faith and public witness. If you walk away from this, it will get you—you will be forced to live two different lives. His witness helped me realize I didn't have to give up the ways my humanity came alive through jazz and comedy. Instead, they were meant to be part of how I follow Christ, preach, and prepare.

This became even clearer to me during the pandemic. In Ohio, we have our governor, Mike DeWine, and all the young adults had something at five o'clock every day called "Wine with DeWine." They would drink wine and watch his updates on the pandemic. In the corner, there was a lady doing sign language. I don't know sign language, and it struck me that it was pretty comical to watch if you don't know it. You have no idea what's happening, but if you did, you'd realize something meaningful was being conveyed. There was a message, but you didn't know the signs. Later on, I read some Albacete things. He gave a talk about romance and how we've lost the connection between romance and the signs of reality. Romance, he said, is meant to be a sign of the infinite. It conveys something more than itself – it leads us somewhere. If we understand life as a series of signs, we wake up because now there's meaning, a destiny we haven't yet reached, and we want more.

Albacete showed us that, often in very comical ways. I never got to meet the guy, but he's still at work. His writings and friendships continue to speak and awaken things in me that I'm grateful for. I realize there aren't two worlds; there aren't two of me. There's just one. And as God said, it's very good. Thank you. [*audience applause*]

Sanchez: Thank you, Fr. Ryan. We're left with a little bit of time, and this is the best part. They always said Albacete liked to answer questions off the cuff. They also said he could tell if the person was paying attention based on their questions. So let's see if I was paying attention! One thing that strikes me about Lorenzo is that, here I am, president of the Albacete Forum, almost 10 years after his death, and we have 70 people committed to continuing his work. The director of the documentary is in the front row there, Fr. Ryan. By the way, there was a *Frontline* documentary.

Mann: Sorry—way to go. Good job. (audience laughter)

Sanchez: There's an incredible capacity in some people to stay awake for us, right? I guess I would ask all of you, first – other than a nostalgic memory of a person, like when we tell great stories of our grandpa who passed away years ago, or war stories – is there an aspect of Lorenzo that is still present? How does that get lived? You know, when you're the child of someone, you carry their name in a certain sense, right? So what does it mean for Lorenzo to still have the capacity to wake us up today? This is for anyone who wants to try that.

O'Malley: Well, for those of us who were lucky enough to enjoy his company and conversation, and experience his great love for people and for the Church—he was really a man of the Church. He had such a wonderful way of taking the Church's Magisterium and making it alive, connecting it to people's lives. It came from a heart transformed by a life of faith and a desire to share the joy of the Gospels with others. As a priest, I think it's important for me to be reminded of that — that having received the Gospel is a responsibility, a responsibility to share that joy with others. In many ways, Lorenzo's example and friendship still touch my ministry. I'm so grateful to you and the others in the Albacete Forum who are trying to pass that on to others as well. Thank you.

Mann: I think it was St. Paul VI who said something like, "The world doesn't listen to teachers anymore, but to witnesses." Lorenzo was such a strong witness that every story you hear about him is captivating. His enduring effect is like the Gospels themselves — he put flesh on it for us. It wasn't just words; it was the Word made flesh. He showed us what that looked like, what it felt like, what it sounded like. He never believed in looking away from the world or your experience to find the Lord. I found that incredibly captivating and healing.

Regarding the 9/11 documentary, his point wasn't that Jesus isn't in the tragedy; it's that you don't need to look away. The light shines in the darkness. It doesn't get rid of it. The Gospel says it shines in it. He's on the cross; He's in the suffering. So, it's more of an invitation to be open, more and more. Lorenzo was a man who lived totally open. That's both captivating and scary, hard and beautiful. All those things come together, and you see them lived out. You see their effect in the lives of his friends. I think that leaves a lasting imprint, like a boat's wake tugging you along. It helps you begin to look at it and practice those things in your own life, to say, "Yeah, this really is a way to be human that is satisfying."

Grygiel: Thank you. As has been said, he loved life in its entirety, with everything that came with it, and he found joy in it. That's why I think he was capable of, for example, sitting at a kid's table pretending to have high tea with a bunch of toddlers while the adults were talking at another table. I wasn't a toddler yet, but for him, that wasn't playful — it was the most natural thing to do, to have a semi-serious conversation with six-year-olds. Right? But that's life, and he was truly curious about it.

One last thing I'll mention that I learned from him: he often would speak and do this [makes a gesture]. You know, right? I used to wonder, "What is that? Is it a nervous tic?" Then he explained, "That's the serpent from The Far Side." He said, "Before original sin, the serpent wasn't crawling. He was standing up." I have no idea what else he drew from that, but it stuck with me. I even used it once in a class on international relations, but it didn't go well because nobody knew what The Far Side was—a different generation! Anyway, he was a great witness in many ways. As a teacher, though, well... he might not always show up to class. A different story. [*audience laughter*]

Sanchez: Thank you. [*audience applause*] In life, I shared a lot with Lorenzo, but what I shared the most was our love for food – and girth. When he met me, he said, "Finally, someone has come to this Movement who's fatter than me!" [*audience laughter*] He said, "There have been all these skinny Italians, and now I feel more like myself." I've always taken that as a great joy.

More than anything, I was with him at the end of his life. What I found was that it didn't matter who entered that hospital room – he felt a great desire to convey love and joy to them. I remember when His Eminence came in at the end of his life, and Lorenzo wasn't there to be pitied. He was grateful, and he wanted to make people laugh, even when he had a tube in his mouth and nose. He had this great capacity to recognize that in the midst of suffering, there was a truth that was more beautiful, rooted in that very suffering.

So, I thank our speakers for sharing today because, for me, Lorenzo continues to keep us awake. On behalf of the New York Encounter, I'd like to thank the Albacete Forum. We exist really as an attempt to keep alive a spirit that, for us, was very much a real friend and continues to offer that friendship to us and to new people all the time. You can visit us at *albaceteforum.org* to find out more. Thank you very much, and thank you to our speakers. [*audience applause*]

TEARING OPEN THE SLEEPING SOUL

WHAT BEAUTY CAN DO TO THE SOUL

A conversation on the power of art to rekindle our humanity, with **Patrick Bringley**, *writer, and* **J.F. Martel**, *author. Moderated by* **Jonathan Fields**, *composer.*

Introduction

A personal encounter with art and beauty can be one of those unpredictable events that awaken us by drawing us nearer to a mysterious "beyond," hidden in everything, and inviting us to start a fascinating journey. Speakers will share their own encounter with art and beauty and how and why it has changed and is still changing their lives.

Jonathan Fields, moderator: Good evening, and on behalf of the Encounter, welcome, everybody—those here at the Metropolitan Pavilion and those following us online. I'm Jonathan Fields, a musician and composer, and I'll be the moderator for this event. I'd like to introduce our two panelists.

Patrick Bringley is the author of *All the Beauty in the World*, a memoir about his decade working as a guard in the galleries of the Metropolitan Museum of Art. The book has been praised in *The New York Times*, *The Washington Post*, *Associated Press*, *Financial Times*, *The Sunday Times* (London), and elsewhere. He's been interviewed by outlets including The *New Yorker*, *The Guardian*, Vox, ABC, CBS, NPR, and BBC. Patrick lives with his wife and children in Sunset Park, Brooklyn, about 10 blocks away from me.

J.F. Martel is a Canadian writer, lecturer, and podcaster. He is the author of *Reclaiming Art in the Age of Artifice*, a book on the power of art published by North Atlantic Press, and forthcoming as an audiobook from Basic Books. As a filmmaker, he has directed French and English documentary series and feature films focusing on art and culture. Martel co-hosts the *Weird Studies* podcast with musicologist Phil Ford.

So, we'd like to begin. I had the great opportunity to read both your contributions to this discussion, "What Beauty Can Do to the Soul." Maybe we could start with you both sharing a little about how you came to write about your experiences and reflections, which we'll be hearing more about today. Patrick, do you want to begin?

Patrick Bringley: Sure. So, right out of college, I got a job at *The New Yorker* magazine. I was just 22 years old, and I thought, "Here I am in a big skyscraper at the corner of 42nd Street and Broadway, I've made it, I'm at the center of things." But while I was there, my brother Tom got sick. He had a soft tissue sarcoma, and it turned out not to be something he was going to beat. Suddenly, I was spending less time in that skyscraper in Midtown and more time in Tom's apartment in Queens and in hospital rooms. It became very clear to me that the most momentous, meaningful things were happening in these quiet little rooms.

When my brother died, I didn't want to rush back to an office job, worrying about office politics or climbing the corporate ladder. I wanted to do something that felt nourishing. I think I was kind of speechless. I wanted to stand still for a while. Remarkably, there's this job — a kind of loophole in the universe — where I could stand still professionally in the most beautiful place I could think of.

As for what brought me to write the book: I spent most of my time at the Met in the old master paintings section. It wasn't lost on me, as I spent these long days with those paintings, that they reminded me of the hospital rooms I had spent time in. You look at these old master paintings—of the Passion, for example (which means "suffering")—and after going through an experience like I did with my brother, you realize those paintings are about the same kinds of things I witnessed in real life. The adoration, the lamentation, the beauty, the pain—it's all there. That experience gave me the confidence to say, "Even though I'm just a guard, I've had experiences that these works of art speak to." I wanted to write about that—not as an expert, but as someone who had meaningful experiences.

J.F. Martel: My story is a bit more prosaic. I've always been involved in art. I grew up playing music, role-playing games (which I consider a form of art), and making films. I wanted to be a filmmaker, but I ended up studying philosophy and history at university because I had that kind of Gen X feeling that you didn't need to go to school to do art; you could do it on your own. After university, I made short films and documentaries for TV in Canada, mostly in French but some in English too. I immersed myself in that industry, which, as you know, is a commercial one.

There was one gig in particular that planted the seed for my book. I took a job with a Montreal company that specialized in big immersive events, involving film, music, and projections. They hired me as a writer for a project to develop an immersive experience for future residents of a gated community in Louisiana. The idea was to create not just a theme-park-like downtown but to provide the residents with a history and mythology for the place. I was creating a hyper-reality for these future residents, and it made me question what I was doing.

I'd always enjoyed the line between me and the artwork—that I could watch a film, then go back to my life. But this idea of living inside an artwork was new to me. It made me reflect on why I started making art in the first place—what moved me as a child. I felt like I was losing touch with that, and I thought the culture was too. So I started researching, thinking, and experimenting, trying to figure out what art really is. It's a question we've all debated, right? "What is art?" Usually, people settle on "It's whatever you call art." But I didn't want to stop there. I wanted to get to the essence of it.

Fields: In reading both your books, I was struck by your incredible passion for beauty. Even though you were working in fields that could be very commercial, you weren't willing to let beauty be just some passing feeling. You both had this relentless desire for beauty to mean something deeply. Patrick, you left a promising career at *The New Yorker*, and J.F., you were working on that kind of bizarre immersive project in Louisiana. So, what kept you both so attached to beauty? Why did you desire it so much that you devoted your lives to it?

Bringley: I mean, I think I'm one of those people who will never stop marveling at the strangeness of existence. If you take a step back and think about what the Metropolitan Museum of Art is, it's this massive temple on Fifth Avenue, filled with things people have made for millennia from every corner of the world. And why do we go there? Maybe an even better question is: why is there enough stuff to fill up a place like that?

I think the reason is because, while we're out in our everyday lives, going about our business, packing kids' lunches, we still have moments where we look around and think, "My God, look at this existence, the beauty of it, the strangeness of it." What is this species I'm a part of? On one hand, I'm just a careless primate, an animal, but on the other hand, I have this mind that seems built to apprehend the beauty, strangeness, and mystery of the universe.

We have these glimmerings, and they need an outlet. We want to sing the song of that or tell stories about it. A place like the Met collects these things that feel sacred to us. Maybe sacred in a literal religious sense, or sacred in the sense of being set apart, which is an old meaning of the word. Sacred from the everyday stuff that seems more disposable. I'm drawn to that. I hope that answers your question.

Martel: It really resonates with me. I think that goes to the core of the aesthetic experience of art, which I explore in my book, *Reclaiming Art in the Age of Artifice*. From the little story I told, you can tell what I'm aiming at: how do we recover a sense of the objective nature of art in an age where it's either diluted by commercial pursuits or considered entirely subjective, a mere social construct? I don't believe it's just a matter of cultural contrivance.

The concept I develop in the book is "radical mystery." It refers to those moments in life when you suddenly awaken to your situation and think, "How strange it is to be here right now." How strange it is that anything exists at all. When you look at someone close to you and see them not as a character in your life, but as a radically different person with their own sense of existence and mystery. Art is about connecting us to that experience. Artworks emerge from that experience.

A great example is Stanley Kubrick's *2001: A Space Odyssey*, where the monolith appears to the hominids, and it imparts something mysterious. The hominid picks up a bone and suddenly envisions using it as a weapon, a leap into what could be — what isn't yet. Art testifies to this human capacity to leap into the imaginal world, the world of possibility, and bring back images of what could be. That necessarily reconnects us with the fundamental mystery of being. We can't fully explain this capacity humans have. Art, technology, tool-building — these things are, in a very real sense, supernatural.

Bringley: On the question of what art is — one nice thing about being a guard at an art museum is that I had lots of time to think about big questions like that. People would ask, "That's armor, or a pot the Greeks used to store olive oil—why is that art?"

One definition I came up with is that art is something that's better than it has any right to be. When you look at a work of art, whether it's more beautiful or more delicate, or more care and skill went into it than we would reasonably expect, it stands out. That's something our species does that other animals don't. Whether it's playing the piano or cooking Italian food, we've gone so far beyond what's necessary. And that excess—pushing beyond what's required—that's what makes art.

Martel: You both touch on the idea that art is completely useless, yet completely necessary. It pulls us out of the pragmatism that insists everything must have a purpose. Art wakes us up to the strangeness and contingency of what we're doing. This table could suddenly become a little stage for someone to dance on.

When you look at the oldest art we have, like the cave paintings in Chauvet, France, some of it was made in hard-to-access parts of the caves where no one would have seen it. Everything they used to make that art — hair from an animal, blood, earth — had a practical purpose, but they repurposed it to create art. Philosophers call it "deterritorializing." That's something unique to our species.

Bringley: Of course, we're getting into the issue of beauty. One interesting thing I observed at the museum is watching people approach a painting and clearly feeling its beauty. You could almost see them being infused with it, but not knowing what to do with that feeling. Sometimes you look at something beautiful, and it's just this fluttering bird in your chest. I'm not sure if "useless" is the right word, but with beauty, you've reached bedrock. You've seen something beautiful, and that's the point — not to write an essay about it, but to experience it. That's why we do this.

Martel: And there's Kant, the philosopher. Kant wrote about this. He said that the experience of beauty is, paradoxically, probably the most subjective experience, the most intimate inner experience—to witness, to see the beautiful—but it manifests itself as an objective fact. You experience beauty as something outside of you, something utterly other. It doesn't feel like an opinion. If you get the experience of seeing beauty, it doesn't feel like you're seeing some kind of projection on your part or something. Now, whether it is that or not is another question, but it feels universal for Kant, which is why it elicits from us an evangelical response. We want to tell other people about it. So, you see a film alone, and you feel like you have to tell someone about it. Someone else has to see this, someone else has to experience this because you know that what you saw wasn't just something you found, but something that was there, waiting for people.

For me, in the book, I say at one point, "Beauty is the quality of things seen for what they really are." I've got some good company here with William Blake, right, who would say to see infinity in a grain of sand. If we could see without the veil of utilitarianism, habit, or reflex—if we could just see the world as it is — it would perhaps strike us as sublimely beautiful. Maybe art is just a matter of framing little bits of the world and polishing them so that the beauty inherent there becomes available to others.

Fields: Obviously, both of you are coming from a great deal of experience in looking at art, and you're also saying that, like the hominids or apes in *2001*, they were able to look at their perceived reality, which informed their creativity. It wasn't an act disconnected from reality. I'd like you to explain a little more about how you learned to look at things, to see art, to the point that it brings you to the truth of reality. It's like a form of knowledge; it's not just an aesthetic experience.

What Beauty Can Do to the Soul

And the other question is, you both brought up that art is not just this beautiful feeling—it's also disturbing. It raises sin, and its being "other" is so radically other. There's also that element to the experience. You both used the word "chaos" at times in relation to art. Could you speak to those two questions that I don't quite remember myself?

Bringley: Oh, sure. I mean, you can get better at it, like anything. But what's interesting about getting better at looking at works of art is that, in some ways, you get better at it by becoming more naive than you were before. I think a lot of people go into an art museum, and they'll know a little about art. So, they see a Rubens picture, and they say, "Okay, that's Baroque, and I know he's got the fleshy people." As a result, you just see that—you see the knowledge you've learned from a textbook or elsewhere. But in reality, the Rubens picture is so much more than that. It's pigment, movement, detail; it's these almost unsophisticated aspects of the world, just the pure beauty of the movements, the line, and everything else.

In a way, the first thing you have to do is nothing—a whole lot of nothing. When you're looking at the picture, you have to watch it almost like television. Watch the thing unfold, have an element of passivity in yourself. Later, you can bring your intelligent mind to the process and think about what you've learned in books. But then, hopefully, you'll go away and come back, and when you come back, you'll start again with that sort of mindset: "Let me give this thing the space to operate on me." It's a never-ending process.

Fields: Did you look at art this way before your brother's illness? Does suffering have something to do with it? I know you both walk around astonished, in wonder, and some of the other talks today touched on the understanding of our wounds, which is also the theme of the Encounter. What I'm asking is, did your way of looking change because of that event? Did you need to see more than what your mind was trying to do to solve this huge, wounded problem?

Bringley: All these things kind of converged at once for me. I had this very shell-shocked experience, and then I got this job, where I was plopped into a museum and told to be quiet for 40 hours a week for 10 years. At the same time, I was becoming a grown-up — I was 25, I got married, and all these things intertwined. I was very lucky to mature inside this museum. Absolutely, all of these experiences influenced how I look at art. I had the privilege of time. Now, when I go to the Met, I have more of a metabolism than most, but if I see a new exhibit, I'll spend three hours there, and then I need to do something else. I have to respond to emails or do something. But in that museum, it was almost monastic — I was told to do none of that. I was told to just exist in this quiet space.

Fields: It's amazing to think that there are still things in this world that exert that type of power over us.

Martel: When we talk about beauty, I find it's a fraught word. It's difficult to talk about beauty. It took me a long time to even see that word pop up in my notes because I was afraid of it. Modern art has largely turned its back on the ideal of beauty. But, as it turns out, I think we've gone through modernism far enough to realize that the great art of the modernist period wasn't so much against beauty as it was about finding new forms of beauty. There was a lot of experimentation and exploration, and I think there were good reasons for it.

But beauty is hard to write about because, in a sense, we're surrounded by a type of beauty, and this is where the dichotomy of art and artifice becomes useful. Milan Kundera calls it kitsch — the idea that there's a type of beauty that confirms what we already expect or think, what we hope the world will be. That type of beauty is not what I'm talking about when I mention Bruegel's harvesters, Shakespeare's *Hamlet*, or a poem by Emily Dickinson. These three things, which have nothing in common with one another, share a certain charge — a weirder type of beauty that's compelling and fascinating. You mentioned the sacred earlier, and Rudolf Otto, the theologian, said that the sacred always manifests in a weird two-pronged way: as a *mysterium tremendum et fascinans* — a terrible and fascinating mystery.

So, when you perceive the sacred, which is how I qualify the type of beauty I'm thinking of, it feels both compelling and fascinating but also a little scary, a little intimidating, a little alien, because of that otherness I mentioned earlier. Rilke wrote about beauty in the first elegy of the *Duino Elegies*. He says, "Who, if I cried out, would hear me among the angels' orders? And even if one of them pressed me suddenly to his heart, I'd be consumed in his more potent being. For beauty is nothing but the beginning of terror, which we can still barely endure, and while we stand in wonder, it coolly disdains to destroy us."

To me, the experience of beauty is an experience of a limit — a limit where I end, and something else begins. That's what's beautiful. But as Hegel said, you can't perceive a limit without imagining yourself on the other side of it. At the same time, my humanity becomes manifest to me as I perceive this limit. As you say beautifully at the end of your book, art does two strange things at once. It reminds us how simple and plain life is. We understand suffering is suffering, stones are stony, and the world is available to us in some strange way — it's very accessible and knowable. But at the same time, in that very knowability, the world becomes strange, endowed with a weird intelligence. That's what I think Rilke means by "angels." An angel isn't just a person with wings — it's an intelligence that's not human and yet active in the world. I think the experience of beauty always involves, or is at least haunted by, this sense of another intelligence at work.

You look at Van Gogh's famous painting, *Wheatfield with Crows*. You see crows flying over a wheat field at dusk. We're getting an image that reflects Van Gogh's state of mind at the end of his life. But he's not showing us himself — he's showing us something out in the world. He's telling us there's a connection between these crows, the wheat, the sky — that all of it adds up to something, somehow.

In one part of your book, you talk about looking at a Chinese scroll covered in calligraphy. You can't read Chinese, but you say — and I love this — that not knowing the language conferred a certain advantage. You could see the language as purely aesthetic, but also as language. That goes to the heart of the artistic experience: both the experience of the artist creating and the experience of us, who are called to receive the art. Through art, we see the world as a script, a text, but the text is written in a language we don't know. We know it's a language, but we can't decipher it. But knowing that it's a language, we cannot help but continue to try to interpret it. That's why a text like *Hamlet* is as pregnant with meaning and open to interpretation today as it was 500 years ago. These are truly magical objects that invite us to engage with our own existence and with the objective nature of the world in a way that I think we're at risk of forgetting today.

Fields: It also seems to mean that art reveals things as they really are, but they're not. We don't want to possess them. We want to possess reality, but art does something else. It creates a space where possession is not your first interest; perhaps observation is. Spirit, contemplation, communion. And that's the other thing — it's this communion that art seems to have the possibility to connect us with. Which brings me to this question: We just saw a dialogue trying to help us understand the position of what's happening in Gaza and someone helping us understand the position in Israel. It's pointing to an irreconcilability at a certain level. But looking is a beginning. How can art speak to this in a world where there is terrible violence, wars, and suffering in our daily lives? How can art be something we even want to do in front of these difficulties? What relevance does it have in the face of what's going on?

Bringley: You can't get away from art because art is also storytelling, it's music, and it's theater. It's kind of every sort of expressive element of what it is to be human. I mean, yes, some of us might believe there's an objective reality out there; some of us might not. But as we explain our view on that reality to one another, we are shaping it. We are creating something. It's a creative act for us to explain ourselves. And then there's the whole side of beauty. The side of beauty we've mostly been speaking about is this almost numinous type of beauty — you look at it, and it feels hard, bright, and irreducible. But there's also the beauty of your family life with your kids, even though it's messy, even though your apartment is strewn with toys, you recognize that there's something beautiful about what you're doing. You feel that you're living a life that is good, for whatever reason.

Fields: So, beauty beyond just looking at art.

Bringley: One hundred percent. I think art can infuse our lives and make us have a broader-minded view. I mean, one thing that's wonderful about the Met, just in terms of talking about geopolitical affairs, is that you go there, and you're reminded of how old the world is — how big, how diverse, and how full of so many different things. You see how many inversions there have been in history. You know, to someone painting a picture of the crucifixion in 14th-century Italy, the idea that the East was a sort of colonized state and that he, in the grand Imperial West, would have found that ridiculous. At that time, the East was so wealthy compared to the pestilent pit of mud where he was painting in Italy. And a place like the Met can remind you of the breadth of existence. I think an understanding of that goes a long way in healing many political wounds — whether it's about whatever everyone's talking about on Twitter or the case of the day — just realizing the breadth of what we're dealing with here.

Martel: The artistic experience, the aesthetic experience, reminds you that what you might otherwise think is just the necessary way things are is actually completely contingent. And by contingent, I mean it could have been otherwise. You think, "Well, this is what a person does in the morning, and that's how one does this, and that's how one does that." But art shows you radically different ways of living that have been preserved in these artifacts, made available to us. It reminds you, like you said, of these long stretches of time. It diffuses, or de-escalates a little bit, the pressures of your time. This doesn't mean there aren't urgent matters to take care of today. But to me, wondering why we make art in a time such as ours... people made art in times that were unimaginably difficult by our terms. The Emperor of Byzantium lived a life that, to us, would seem extremely miserable, right? Just due to the lack of basic infrastructure. That's one thing. War has been a constant, and somehow humans have always found it necessary to make art. To me, saying that we should stop making or enjoying art because there are more pressing matters is to interpret art as a form of entertainment, which I don't think it is. Entertainment comes from the French word *entretenir*, which means "to maintain." So when you hear entertainment, you should hear maintenance, right? It's not just entertainment. Wait, where was I? Instead of seeing art as a form of entertainment... I've lost my thought.

Bringley: Art's good. Art's good. [*audience laughter*] People ask for advice on visiting the Met, and I always give twofold advice. Art can be very humbling, and it can also be very inspiring. I think in any given visit to the Met, one thing you can do is show up in the morning when it's quiet and first just wander. Feel tiny, like you're staring up at the nighttime stars and realizing everything in your head could not mean less — it's just nonsense, even what's going on in this country or this world. Look at how huge existence is. There's something very cleansing and beautiful about that. But then at some point, you flip a switch and say, "Well, I'm looking at this Greek statue, and this thing's made out of stone. But I'm made out of marvelous cells. I'm a living thing." You puff out your chest and think, "Well, the Greeks were human. I'm human. I can think thoughts about the nature of the universe, the nature of death, life, suffering, the gods, and everything else." Use the art as fuel and think creative thoughts yourself. In the same way that beauty teaches us something about the great plainness of things and the great mystery of things, art is both humbling and emboldening.

Martel: I remember what I wanted to say. [*audience laughter*]

Bringley: That's the whole reason I did that. [*audience laughter*]

Martel: Asking why we make art when there are such urgent matters to take care of is like asking an athlete why she's wasting calories beating her heart instead of just training. It's the heartbeat. Art is not something you do in order for something else to happen. Art, to me, is the sign that things are going well — that the body of society is functioning, that your culture is developing. When we stop making art, the urgency of all those other matters will cease to be, because nothing will matter. Art is the search for meaning. It's the way through which humans express and search for that meaning. It's easy in this conversation to think we're talking about pictures at the Met or pieces of music, but really, in a sense, those are just artifacts that have emerged from this universal process by which humans search for meaning. The artifacts are just signs that humans are doing this thing. We're all doing this thing in our own way. We're all searching in our own way. And as they say, "Seek and you shall find."

Fields: I just saw the Grammys. You know, I watched the Grammys, and it's very easy to be cynical now, thinking, "Oh my god, it's all artifice, it's just entertainment, right? Maintenance." But art manages to break through. When Tracy Chapman played *Fast Car* with Luke Combs, it transfixed me. Suddenly, this huge thing that seemed to have nothing to do with art or the heart beating became a moment. It's as if everything outside tries to reduce everything, but then, if one human being is able to make that thing happen and communicate it, all the rest of the stuff just disappears because it's so real. Yeah, exactly. And that moment — I couldn't believe that moment, because I'm so cynical, you know? And then that happens. So it's still happening somehow.

Bringley: I think that's how it's always been. We were joking before about something I quote in my book — Michelangelo complained, saying, "This age is hostile to our arts." And the age he meant was the High Renaissance. [*audience laughter*] I think that's how it's always been. Of course, Michelangelo wasn't aware it was the High Renaissance. He wasn't aware of himself as some sort of colossus of art history. He was a guy who went to work every day, dealing with the unbelievable rewards, but also the frustrations of having money pulled out from under him, the pope changing his mind, client problems, etc.

Art is created by people who are hemmed in by circumstances, sometimes very, very tightly. Certainly, if you study the history of art, a lot of the wonderful things we're talking about weren't made by free individuals who had a beautiful studio in Soho or something. They were made by Greek or Egyptian craftsmen who were basically serfs working for the Pharaoh.

Fields: You both speak about making art, and you talk about the day's work. You also talk about having to maintain a sense of awe, this astonishing, original wonder, but then you also have to get down to the hard work of doing. You both spoke about writing your books, dealing with editors, the comments, and all that. Somehow, they both go together. How do you maintain this need for art and, at the same time, manage the incredible, intense craft it requires? You know, my boss used to tell me, "You've edited so much, you've taken every bit of music out of it."

Martel: You have a vision, an idea, a feeling that you want to express, right? And then you start to work on it. So, what do you need? Well, you need a medium. Is it going to be a song? For most artists, that's not really a question because they're already devoted to a medium. But for me, as a dabbler, I had to pick the medium for an idea, or sometimes the idea picks the medium. But the point is, you need a medium. You need to work some kind of material into the artifact. Then you need tools. Then you need skills, and skills have to be developed over time.

It won't do to just process it through some kind of AI because what you're trying to convey is not just a form but an experience, something very deeply personal. You can't just be like Neo in *The Matrix*, saying, "I know kung fu." You have to learn kung fu, you know? So, you go through this process, trying not to lose sight of that original vision, that original idea. It's very difficult. Any editing or revision that happens must be done in the spirit of that initial insight.

Now, I'm putting it in simplistic terms, and any working artist here would have their own way of explaining this process. It's as varied as the people creating art. But I think, in essence, that's what you're trying to do with art: you're trying to perform a kind of miracle. You're trying to take something purely imaginal and give it a material form, whether that material is vibrations composing a song, a film, a painting, a sculpture, or a novel. You're trying to give material form to something immaterial, and that's not easy. So it's true that artists have always complained about this process, but we can try to create a society that encourages that sort of work, right? By having a polity that appreciates art and also putting in place the structures and processes that allow people to feel encouraged to make art. That's why the age we're in, with AI, holds great promise but also great dangers for that reason.

Fields: Would you like to have the final word?

Bringley: Oh, sure. You were talking about trying not to lose sight of the thing that animates you, and you lose sight of it every day. This process is one of losing sight of the thing, then regaining it, and losing sight again. I think that's one thing art helps us with—it helps us remember. Often, art teaches us something we already know. It's not always sophisticated or wordy; it's something like "suffering is real" or "the universe is beautiful." It's something we know, but we drift from it as we get caught up in the weeds of our profane lives. Art brings us back. It's like a warm hug.

Martel: There's a Russian critic who said, "Art is about making the stone stony." It's as simple as that.

Fields: I think the synthesis of all this is: art is good. [*audience laughter*] I'd like to thank our guests. [*audience applause*]

What Beauty Can Do to the Soul

MADE TO BE FREE

A conversation on education in light of Fr. Luigi Giussani's pedagogy with **Hans van Mourik Broekman***, principal of Liverpool College, U.K., and* **Aaron Riches***, professor of theology, Benedictine College in Atchison, KS. Moderated by* **Amy Hickl***, dean of faculty, Notre Dame Academy School, Los Angeles.*

Introduction

Fr. Giussani, the Italian priest who founded the international Catholic movement of Communion and Liberation, has been known to be an educator, able to communicate the faith in a persuasive way to many young people through an original pedagogical approach and method. Can his educational proposal work outside of the Italian system and at a different time, marked by a heavily ideological context? If so, why and how? Speakers are teachers who are familiar with Fr. Giussani's pedagogy and will address these questions through their first-hand experience with high school and college students.

Amy Hickl, moderator: Hello, everyone. Welcome. On behalf of the New York Encounter, thank you for being here. We welcome both those who are with us in the pavilion and those joining us online. I'm Amy Hickl, a teacher and administrator at a school in Los Angeles, California, and I'll be moderating this event today. Before we begin, I'd like to thank Benedictine College in Atchison, Kansas, for helping us organize this great event.

One of the claims of our theme this year for the Encounter is that the signs we see in ourselves and around us — this uneasiness, this loneliness, this sadness — reveal something irreducible in the human being: the desire for beauty, for justice, for home, for truth, and so on. According to Fr. Giussani, to understand this and to begin to address it is, first and foremost, a problem of education. He believed that in order to regain a gusto for life — what he called "the taste for living" — we need to enter into reality and discover what makes that possible. And he insists that, for this, we need to be educated. This is the heart of what education is.

I'm a teacher and an administrator, and I was not taught this in teacher school. For us, it's about the skills and knowledge students need to acquire. So, coming across the work of Fr. Giussani and the way he talks about education is deeply fascinating for me. Today, we have with us two friends who are very familiar with this pedagogy, and they will help us unpack and explore it further.

First, we have Hans van Mourik Broekman, the principal of Liverpool College, a school for children ages 4 to 19 in the heart of Liverpool. Hans is a native of the Netherlands. He attended high school in the U.S. and earned his master's degree with honors in Classics from the University of St. Andrews in Scotland. After teaching in the UK, Hans returned to the U.S., where he served as Deputy Headmaster, Headmaster, and Principal in Washington, DC, Arkansas, and Tennessee. In July 2007, he was appointed the 17th principal of Liverpool College and took up the role in June 2008. The school, which once primarily served wealthy citizens of Liverpool, now reflects in its student body every ethnic background, every advantage and disadvantage, every faith tradition, and every country of origin found in inner-city Liverpool. Hans was instrumental in making this happen, and in November 2019, the school was awarded an outstanding rating in all areas by the National School Inspectorate. So, we welcome Hans.

We also have with us Aaron Riches, an Associate Professor of Theology at Benedictine College. Aaron was born in Canada and completed his doctoral studies in England at the University of Nottingham. After almost a decade teaching at the major seminary of the Archdiocese of Granada in Spain, he took up his current position at Benedictine in Atchison, Kansas, where he lives with his wife and six children. So, welcome, Aaron, and thank you both for being here.

I want to start by asking both of you how you came across Fr. Giussani. Hans, I know you have a particularly interesting story. Can you share it with us?

Hans van Mourik Broekman: During COVID, when the school closed and I wasn't working 60 hours a week managing the school, I remembered that on 9/11, our family was traveling back from Europe to the United States, and we were diverted to Canada, to Moncton. We were eventually rescued from an ice hockey rink with our young children by a Canadian family, and in the basement of their house, we just watched CNN, as I think most people were doing. This priest was invited to speak — a rather corpulent priest [*audience laughter*] — and I think you know who I'm talking about. He was amazing. It was brief, but he was very honest. He said, "I know these acts come from religion because I recognize this passion in myself."

So, when COVID struck, I was bicycling along the Mersey River, and I thought, "I wonder what that guy would say about COVID." I was going to Google "corpulent priest speaks," but instead, I searched "CNN 9/11 priest." Anyway, I discovered that he had passed away. One of the wonders of the internet is that you're then directed to other videos of him, and there was one that had only been viewed 453 times at the time. A person from a TV network called The Meaning of Life interviewed him for an hour, and it was very obvious that it was a hot summer day. He was in short sleeves, and they were both sweating profusely. I was completely riveted by everything he said. At the very end of the interview, he said, "There's a man that I follow." So, I thought, "Okay, who could that be?" I ordered his books — Amazon was still working throughout the pandemic—and then I discovered a link to Giussani's *The Risk of Education*. I knew I had definitely found something.

At the time, I didn't realize there was a movement. I just knew about the books. And, for those of you who are here, you probably know how difficult it is to get in touch with CL [*audience laughter*]. Eventually, I think I wrote an email in frustration to headquarters in Milan because people were saying, "Well, this guy will call you," but nothing happened. Then

I discovered that my wife was receiving WhatsApp messages from the CL website – from a lady in an adjacent parish in Liverpool – and this was all in the middle of COVID. I began to follow that group, who have since become very close friends of ours. This was about three years ago, something like that.

Hickl: Thank you. And Aaron, how did you first come across Fr. Giussani?

Aaron Riches: I went to the University of Virginia, where I was planning to pursue a PhD, but I left after only two years to follow my professor, John Milbank, to England. After leaving the University of Virginia, John Milbank met some friends in the Comunione e Liberazione (CL) movement in Milan. Various people associated with CL would come to the University of Nottingham, and they took him to the Rimini Meeting. As a result, I got to know some friends in the Movement. However, it wasn't until around 2008 or 2009 that I truly encountered the Movement. One of those friends at the Catholic University in Milan sent a 19-year-old student to the University of Nottingham to finish his undergraduate thesis with John Milbank, and that's when I met the Movement.

This student came up, and my friend in Milan called and said, "Will you look after him? Make sure he doesn't get lost in Nottingham." He showed up, and his name was Michelangelo. He smoked toscanos, drank beer, wore a Rancid T-shirt, and loved playing silly folk songs on the guitar. He walked into our house and just started doing the dishes without being asked. He became really good friends with our one-and-a-half-year-old son. He said to us, "Because I'm part of this thing, CL" – which I had heard of, and I even owned *The Risk of Education* at that point, but unfortunately, I had tried to read it and didn't understand a word. "I do this other thing, which is called School of Community. There's no School of Community in Nottingham, so I'm going to hold a School of Community in your living room, and you and Melissa are invited to come." So we had our first encounter with the Movement in our living room through this 19-year-old kid.

Here's the remarkable thing: at that time, I had just gotten my PhD in theology and was starting to adjunct teach at the University of Nottingham. Suddenly, here was this 19-year-old undergraduate, and his gusto for life and ability to engage fully with all aspects of life was something I had never encountered before. I converted to Christianity when I was 27 years old, and there was a clear before and after in my life — not necessarily theoretically, but in the way I lived. I felt a kind of fracture in my life, with many parts I wanted to push aside or ignore. He came along, and he was really into anarchism, Trotskyism, punk rock, playing guitar, and morning prayer. The experience of being around him was transformative. I mean, this is education, right? Here was this 19-year-old authority figure, and I was a 30-something-year-old with a PhD in theology, yet he gave me back to myself. He made my life whole just by being around him.

We participated in the School of Community, and we went to an encounter with Caron in 2008 or 2009. Eventually, he returned to Italy and became a monk at the Cascinazza Monastery, where he still is today.

Hickl: Thank you. That's great. [*audience applause*] So, education: we want to learn math and how to write essays and all of that, but we also want that taste for living. Hans, you've shared before that when you read *The Risk of Education* during that time period, you had, by all accounts, a highly successful school with numerous accolades — this was the ideal as an educator. Yet after reading *The Risk of Education*, you said, "We have to change some things around here." Can you talk to us about what was missing and what Fr. Giussani had?

Broekman: Well, he had life. He had a vision of education that far exceeds the regulatory framework of British state education. It's not difficult to surpass that, but this exceeds it in an exponential fashion. My experience of reading that book was, "This is true. This is true." I then remembered, as our friends from Ireland would say, when you ask for directions, "Don't start from here."

I looked at the school I was leading. It is a secular school that accepts children from every background and faith tradition. The most active faith tradition in my school is, by far, the Muslim students, who engage with me about their beliefs all the time. But I could see right away that what Giussani was saying — that something true is true everywhere — applies to my school as well. The practical implications of this were twofold.

First, I realized that in our school, it was not possible for students to form meaningful relationships. An English kid might have about 15 different teachers and see each one only two or three times a fortnight. So, we made a change that enabled a group of young people to spend time with one teacher over several years for three and a half to four hours a week, doing activities like playing the ukulele – something your friend from Milan would have approved of. We almost invented a series of what we called "learning opportunities," and when the bureaucrats got hold of this during inspections, they said we had an excellent personal development program.

We found something we could expand on that inspired people to think much more broadly about education. The other change was in pedagogy, the actual teaching methods. The British government is obsessed with the quality of questioning in the classroom, and I definitely saw an opening there. I think the question, "What does this mean?" is seldom asked in school. It's such an easy thing to introduce when teaching: asking students what something means, starting from their own experiences. This was a dramatic pedagogical change.

The government's vision of an English teacher is like a petroleum transfer engineer. Yet our regulator defines knowledge as a permanent change in the brain, which is a very reductive view. By simply asking students questions like, "What does this mean? What do you want? Why do you want that? Is this true in your experience?" we can engage them in a way that's never been done in an English school before. You'd be amazed at the effect that this has.

So, just these two very simple things in a constrained situation – where we may not be able to do all the things we want – made a significant impact. By emphasizing these two aspects, we changed the curriculum and the way we questioned students. We always tried to relate what they were learning to the bigger picture by asking, "What does this mean?" I think those were the key changes we made.

Hickl: Aaron, do you find that as well? This question of, "What does this mean? How does it relate to my life?" Do you find that need in your students?

Riches: Yeah. I mean, I think that the question, "How does this relate to me in my life?" is essential. I can say that it came up for me as an educator.

The first classes I taught were before I knew anything about the Movement. I had this book, *The Risk of Education*, which I didn't fully understand. I taught classes in Christology and other subjects at the University of Nottingham. However, when I went to Spain, I faced a problem: I didn't really know Spanish, and I was put in front of seminarians and had to teach them. That was incredibly awkward.

There's a coincidence here, right? It turned out that I had more practice speaking Spanish at School of Community in Spain than I did anywhere else. The other thing, too, is that if you don't know the language very well, you have to ground everything really deeply in experience to convey anything of importance. When speaking in your own language, it's easy to let the words fly and thoughts wander, losing the grounding completely.

So, I discovered that in order to propose anything to my students, I really had to start with my own life, my own circumstances, and something that happened to me today – an event I witnessed on the way to work. The seminarians really responded to that. Now, it's not that the movement wasn't present in the seminary; in fact, it was there because I had been invited to teach by Archbishop Javier Martinez of Granada, who has a deep history in the Movement. But I think there was a newness in the way I taught, stemming from a place of complete fragility, where the only thing I had to hold on to was my own experience. I've followed that into my teaching now at Benedictine College, where I try to start from that place. I don't always succeed; I'm just as susceptible to abstractions as anyone else, but that's why I try to begin there.

Hickl: I want to touch on this idea of authority, as you both have discussed it in various ways. If my role as an educator, parent, or adult is not just to transmit knowledge, we still need authority – a word that is highly charged these days. Help us understand Fr. Giussani's idea of what authority is, why it's important, and how one can be an authority for their students or children.

Riches: The first way to answer the question is that Fr. Giussani says authority comes from the Latin term meaning "that which lets something grow." To truly have authority involves making a real, concrete proposal that has been made flesh and blood in me to another person. In a certain sense, you accompany them, but at the same time, you also step back to let it take root in the other person.

My experience is that I bring a certainty to the classroom that has been verified, and when I propose it, the more I do so with life — flesh and blood, fullness, and examples from my own life, including my fragilities and mistakes — the more it becomes something the student can approach. The more they can approach it, the more they start to verify it themselves. The miracle, for me, is that it grows into a certainty within them. Then I can follow them, becoming the pupil, and they the educator. This circularity is what authority means to me. Authority is not something I can hold on to; it's something I have to try to generate in another person, giving them the tools to generate it within themselves so that I can step back and let them be the authority for me.

Hickl: Put a little more flesh on this for us. For example, you mentioned earlier that you had your students read the biography of Fr. Giussani in class. It's quite a lengthy book, right? Tell us about that.

Riches: It was kind of a stupid idea. [*audience laughter*] The book is too big to read in an undergraduate or high school class. I did it because I wanted to read the biography, but also because I thought that if you pick up *The Risk of Education*, it's hard to read. However, starting with the life of this man makes sense — it's not that it's easy, but it provides context. The journey he made is what makes this book important. I wanted to explore the things he looked at, hear the sounds he heard, and understand what gave him life and generated this whole Movement.

So, I proposed this class, and the students actually seemed to enjoy it. The most incredible moment for me was at the end of the class when I said, "Okay, this is what we're going to do for the final examination." They were all worried, asking, "When's the final exam? Dr. Riches, are you going to give us the question in advance?" I said, "No, the final exam is this: in the Movement, we do a thing called the assembly, and that's your final exam." Each student had to speak.

I'll read you one response from a student, which I find beautiful. I asked them what they took away from the class, seeking a synthesis of what was most important for them. One student said, "Towards the end of his life, when he was really sick, there was a day when he was in great pain. He said, 'In my condition, I have very little life left, but until my last breath, my first feeling is gratitude, because it comes from him.'" Oh gosh! She added, "I didn't think the thing that would strike me from this book would be gratitude," pointing at how thick the book is. [*audience laughter*]

She continued, "I've never had this understanding of gratitude before. Reading about Giussani and seeing how he views others with gratitude — how he sees people as a gift — was the thing that struck me the most. You can see it from the very beginning of the book, the way he talks about his father, who was a socialist. He acknowledges his imperfections, but what he remembers is the gift he received from his father. He does this repeatedly, whether in hard situations or beautiful ones. He possesses the certainty that what's given to him is truly a gift. Giussani saw this gift in the nurses around him, in his friends, and in people he barely knew. He approached them as if they were a gift, solely for him. It doesn't mean he wasn't aware of their imperfections, but he focused on the good things — not just the good things, but the good things as gifts, meaning he saw the destiny shining through them.

The thing I want to take away, what I will take away from this class, is that I, too, want to see everything as a gift. I've never been so thankful. That doesn't mean things aren't hard, but the more I lose, the more thankful I become. So, if I ever forget, remind me that this was my experience." [*audience applause*]

Now, this is a kid whose experience of the Movement, even though they attended Benedictine College, was not immersed in CLU or the charism. They just happened to be in a capstone theology class with me. That's where the verification happened. I want to follow that person.

Broekman: I just wish I'd met him and his example a lot earlier. I think when you have a vocation to be an educator, and you become aware of somebody like Fr. Giussani, it's a standard. It's a judgment. I had the privilege of staying in Milan. CL said, "She lives on the fifth floor. Ring the bell. Someone will open the door. You will stay there." And she turned out to be a person who was in his first class in 1954. So, as an educator and also as a principal — I've been a principal for 26 years — and a father for about the same amount of time, Giussani's understanding of authority is something that I wish I'd had much earlier in my life.

In my setting, a secular one, this is something that everybody I work with acknowledges as true. You know, why is this teacher so effective? Why is this person having an impact on young people? Which is what we, as educators, want to achieve. Why is this person the place where this growth is happening? Well, because they're witnesses to something beyond themselves. They are not trying to do this on their own.

Hickl: Aaron, we were talking about witness earlier too. Fr. Giussani says, at a certain point, all education is a witness. You're witnessing to something.

Riches: What does the witness witness to? I mean, the witness witnesses to Christ, who is the teacher, but he's more than just the teacher because he's also the principal point at which, if I look at him, everything takes on meaning. One of my favorite quotes in this book is actually the quotation that Giussani makes of Romano Guardini when he says, "In the experience of a great love, everything becomes a factor in its orbit." If I can have that experience of a great love of Christ, who is the real teacher and the point at which life is truly given, then even the disaffections and frustrations can be understood within that point of irreducible positivity.

So the educator, I think, to bear witness must show that life is good, that the world we live in is good, that the moment of history I'm in now — even though it might be overwhelming at times — is good, and it's good that I'm here. He says, you know, fix your point. Fix your eyes on that one point of positivity. You know, Leonard Cohen said, "The crack is where the light shines through." That's the point at which you see the truth, and all the other factors take on consistency. Giussani says, quoting from the Gospel of John, "He loved his own in the world, and he loved them to the end."

And this is really what tradition is, right? We can think about tradition as being all kinds of ideas, but really, the real tradition is that Jesus gives himself, right? He gives himself, and on the night in which he's betrayed, he hands on his presence. That's the core of the Christian tradition. And the journey, he says, that the educator and pupil are called to take together is the journey of explicitly running the risk of accepting the call and the challenge of this definition of ourselves. This definition of myself is one who's loved so much that God enters into the world and dies for me, who takes on all the negativity of my life, the frustrations, and meets me there. "Whither shall I flee from thy spirit?"

And then he says that this is how the mystery invites us to recognize ourselves as made by him — that I'm made from this mercy, this mercy that will chase me to the bottom of hell if it has to. This is what I want to bear witness to, right? And it is in this common journey — the common journey of the educator and the pupil who keep on switching spots — defined by the definitive endpoint of the Destiny who came into the world to find me, even in the bottom of hell or in my worst failure. It's at this point that we come to know the features of our path. And that's the gospel, right? That's to announce the gospel. It's to bear witness to this reality: that it happened, that he really did this, that God took on my negativity and found me there.

Hickl: Thank you. So, you were also touching on this point: the educator is one who bears witness that life is good and, as you were saying, there's something that takes on the frustrations, the negative experiences, and can sustain the young person through those. Fr. Giussani says it's absolutely critical that this role of verification and criticism be present. If I'm going to become an adult, I have to take the ideas that have been given to me in my tradition, sift through them, and take them up as my own. He speaks in a very particular way about criticism — not as something cynical or negative, but as something essential and important. Can you help us unpack that a little bit more?

Riches: What Giussani doesn't mean is what Karl Marx refers to when he talks about "ruthless criticism of all things existing" as a kind of negative thing to uncover hidden agendas. That's a form, I think, for Giussani, of skepticism. Giussani's understanding of "criticism" is an opening up. He has that image of the backpack, where the parent or educator puts things into the child's backpack, and at a certain point, the child starts taking the things out of the backpack to see how they work. This is the most beautiful point because it's where the educator really has to step back and not micromanage what the young person is doing, which is finding the things that are useful for them.

Because it matters not at all if I believe that Christ was raised on the third day in the abstract. What matters is that I see where it touches my life in flesh and blood. So the witness, the educator, has to, when proposing, give examples from their own life. It's no use to give examples from other people's lives. It has to be your own life. Where is it? Where is it flesh and blood for you?

Then the student or pupil takes these tools out of their backpack and looks to see how they work, if they work. There's the freedom to say yes or no, but I almost want to say — and I think Giussani would agree with this — it's not even a matter of saying yes or no. It's the quality of the yes or no that you say. There's a certain kind of "no" when it's finding that it's not working that's still sincere. The question is whether the student is sincere when they're trying to figure out whether this tradition works in life, whether it's useful. You can still have something to work with if the "no" is said from sincerity.

But of course, in the "yes" too — saying yes in a placid way wouldn't be helpful, but to say yes with a full-blooded searching — that's what we want to achieve, and that involves letting the other be free.

Hickl: Hans, what would you say?

Broekman: Well, the first insight I would have is that I think the concept of tradition is too focused on the past. I think, inevitably, in educational and ecclesial terms, when you use that word, you're inviting people to take a position in relation to a cultural canon or a religious canon.

Of course, the tradition is also about the future. I think I read something from Pope Benedict talking about that. My experience with pupils is that if I start going on about the tradition or my tradition, in my school people would say, "Well, this is my tradition." You know, whose tradition? Whose virtue? Whose value? But if we think of criticism as the fundamental judgment that is at the heart of all education from our experience, again, I think we're in danger of mystifying this a little bit. I mean, any educator in this room is going to recognize immediately what we're talking about.

Because ultimately, we learn through judgment against the standard through experience. For us, the judgment is made against the totality that is Christ — the complete moment of judgment. To guide people to understand the ingredient of judgment in their own education is to move away from the conceptions that Aaron mentioned in terms of criticism as destruction or negation. But rather, it's always a yes. Ultimately, our judgment is always a yes, even when the judgment is "no."

I think when an educator is able to present life — the fullness of life, the totality of life—the judgment then becomes about the future. In a sense, it becomes about the path that I do want to take. It steps away from an excessive focus on what Giussani warned against: traditionalism. I think understanding that education is about now. It's about pupils and teachers.

Riches: I think that this emphasis on the present is absolutely key, especially — just to go back to the point I made before — which is that at the core of the tradition is the gift of presence itself: Jesus's own presence. The other point I wanted to mention is this: Giussani bets on the human heart. I mean, the criteria for judgment is in you, and no one else can do that work. That's a great thing to say. There's a little story about Giussani: some kid in Milan becomes a communist, and his parents freak out. They don't know what to do. The dad calls up Fr. Giussani and says, "What are we going to do? Even little kids are joining the Communist Party!" He says, "Just help me over for dinner. I can sort it all out." This reassures the mother, who is clearly worried. Giussani comes over, and he brings a big box. The kid comes out, and he says, "Congratulations! You've made a great move in your life. You've taken a decision that concerns your destiny, life itself, and your pursuit of truth. I brought you this present to celebrate." The kid opens the box in front of his parents and is aghast. It's Leon Trotsky, Rosa Luxemburg, Karl Marx — all the different traditions of Marxism. Giussani says, "We're going to read these books together. If we find what you're looking for in here, then we're going to make the best damn communist out of you that we can. [*audience laughter*] But if what you're really looking for isn't in here, then we'll start again with the proposal of Christianity." That's amazing because he really bets on the kid's heart to find it. He believes they'll find what they need, and he's not going to micromanage it for them. That certainty that Giussani has — that all roads lead to Christ — is obviously overwhelming. The parent who's trying to micromanage what the kid gets involved in betrays a kind of fearfulness that is not certainty.

But when Giussani walks in like that, it's absolute certainty, along with accompaniment and love, betting on the heart of that child that they'll find what they're looking for.

Hickl: That's actually what I wanted to ask you both. These are beautiful insights. But do you have examples or stories from today that can help us see what this verification looks like, with the authority and accompaniment of the student, the child, all the way to certainty? What does it look like in your classrooms as fathers?

Riches: It's a dangerous question, and on this one, I'm definitely going to let Hans go first. [*audience laughter*]

Broekman: I think, you know, when you're a father, you think about this deeply and intensely. When you meet me at my school, you're two steps away from being expelled. This is a large organization with lots of pastoral and academic interventions. When you and your family are in my office, things really are not okay. There could be a policeman in there or a social worker. What I've noticed is that the fundamental question that presents itself in those situations is: Is there any mercy in the world? Is there any tenderness? Is there a possibility of forgiveness? Does this even exist? I deal with people who are interacting with me in a specific role, and I think the challenge for the father is to think more like the educator, and for the educator to think more like the father — to try to be that authority that protects, nourishes, and witnesses to the reality that there is tenderness in the world.

Now, if my students heard me say this, they would say, "Well, that's a load of baloney," because that guy is super strict and punishes. I have this amazing sense in my context that people are unsure whether there is tenderness in the world. In the hierarchy of what we need to do as fathers and educators, we have to make sure that people know there is tenderness in the world, that we have experienced mercy, and that there is forgiveness of all sins. As Aaron has said, the despair that marks a lot of people's experiences in my school is fundamentally a deep concern about whether there's anything good in the world. It's much more severe than people realize.

Riches: Wow, that was really helpful to me. Thank you, Hans, because this formula that the educator needs to be more like a father and the father more like an educator rings so profoundly true to me. It's not something I ever quite thought of, but I see that every once in a while. You know, I'll have a student say, "Oh, you've really been like a father to me," and I think, "Gosh, I've messed up my own kids!" [*audience laughter*] The reason that a father tends to mess up his own kids is obviously faithlessness – a lack of certainty in Christ. So then they parent, or educate, from a position of fear. A friend of mine said to me once, "You can only parent in a human way when you parent from love, never from fear." Those are terrifying words for a parent because most parents do parent from fear a lot.

But I'll just share one very small example of a kind of mystery that happened. I came to a point in my life not too long ago where I thought, with my two eldest kids, I really wanted to apologize for some things I had done as a parent. I sat them down separately – not in a formal way, just in quiet moments – and said, "There are a couple of things I wanted to apologize for." Some of them go way back to when they were kids. For example, I remember I gave a stupid ultimatum: "If you do this again, then I'm going to throw your hot chocolate in the garbage." I was kind of mad, overbearing. Of course, this little kid, old enough to remember, did it again, and I threw it in the garbage. They cried so much that we had to leave the restaurant we were in. I often thought back on that moment and asked myself, "What kind of a dad does that? That was a mistake." I harmed my own kid by doing that.

The joy of this mercy is really that forgiveness is another remarkable gift. This is Christianity: everything flows from mercy. An error, our sin, is God's opportunity. It's almost as if he's glad we sin because now he gets to show us just how much he loves us. When I sin against my own kid, I have to take it that way: this is an opportunity to prove just how much I really love them by humbling myself and saying, "There's this thing that happened, and I'm sorry."

Hickl: Fr. Giussani says something interesting about that, though. He mentions that often we, as the adults, get paralyzed or stuck in this desire to be perfect. Giussani says it's not really about moral coherence – that I always do exactly what I say — but that what is absolutely essential is if I lack coherence with the ideal.

Riches: Well, I mean, his commentary on the *Miserere* from Spirito Gentile at the end states that the ideal of the ideal is *not* to not sin. The ideal is Jesus Christ. If the ideal was to not sin, then it would be like desiring to arrive in front of him and say, "Look, I did it on my own." That means that sin is not an incoherence in and of itself. Pope Francis says that sin is the privileged moment of our encounter with Christ. When we recognize it as sin and name it for what it was, it actually becomes a positive moment.

Broekman: What I see in my colleagues is that coherence comes from fidelity to a vocation — fidelity to the vocation of teaching. The coherence that the pupil experiences comes from that fidelity to the vocation. Every teacher is aware that they're not the teacher they want to be. No one wants to teach all the first years, so they give them to me — sometimes in groups of 100. What I notice is that when I'm not faithful to that vocation, the students know it. They have infallible antennae. It reminds me of a line from the novel *Death Comes for the Archbishop*: "I do not see you as you really are; I see you through my love of you." That's who you are.

So the challenge for the educator is the challenge of affectivity because, fundamentally, the vocation is a vocation to love in all circumstances. The possibility of education occurs, as Aaron has said, in a kind of mutual authority grounded in that love. Fidelity to the vocation is a great conversation to have with my union rep, you know, because they're always going on strike. I say, "Well, we have to be faithful to our vocation. The children have to learn; we can't be on strike all the time." They look at me like, "What are you talking about?"

When you really listen to what teachers, students, and pupils say about their teachers, the coherence they're looking for is fidelity to the vocation.

Hickl: I could keep asking these gentlemen questions all day, but we're coming to the end of our time. I do think that's a good place to leave it, because this mercy and this fidelity are what allow me to be free as an educator, and that allows my students to be free as young learners. So thank you both very much. [*audience applause*]

MADE TO BE FREE

AN INCURABLE WOUND?

Eye-witness accounts of the life of Christians in the Holy Land, with **Alessandra Buzzetti**, *TV journalist in Jerusalem,* **Fr. David Grenier, O.F.M.**, *commissary of the Holy Land for the United States,* **Cardinal Pierbattista Pizzaballa**, *Latin Patriarch of Jerusalem,* **Fr. Gabriel Romanelli**, *pastor of Holy Family Catholic Parish in Gaza, and other Christians from Gaza and the West Bank. Moderated by* **Riro Maniscalco**, *Encounter's president.*

Introduction

There is no lack of daily opinions, comments, and analyses on what has been happening in the Holy Land since October 7, 2023. But what is the experience of Christians living in that tortured region? Is there a distinctive judgment about the war between Israel and Hamas stemming from their faith? Speakers, either in person or via video, will bring their perspective on the day-to-day life in the Holy Land and allow us to look at that reality through their eyes.

Riro Maniscalco, moderator: Good afternoon, everybody, and on behalf of the Encounter, welcome to this presentation. Well, it's more than a presentation. That's how I look at it: sharing seeds of hope where hope is needed the most. We have with us today Alessandra Buzzetti, a journalist who has been living in Jerusalem since 2019 as the Middle East correspondent for TV 2000, an Italian Catholic network. After earning a degree in modern literature, she worked for networks like Swiss Italian

Television, the Italian state TV, and several others. Alessandra is also a writer and author of several books.

To my right, we have Fr. David Grenier, who is the Commissary of the Holy Land for the US. Originally from Canada, he joined the Franciscans of the Custody of the Holy Land in 2007 and was ordained a priest in Jerusalem on June 29, 2015. Fr. David served as the director of the Magnificat Institute, bringing Christians, Jews, and Muslims together through music. He is currently the Secretary of the Holy Land and resides at the Franciscan Monastery of the Holy Land in Washington, DC. I'm Riro Maniscalco, the president of the Encounter. I'm supposed to moderate, but I don't think there's anything to moderate here. There's a lot to embrace, a lot to see, a lot to cry for, and hopefully, a lot to hope for.

That's why I'll ask Alessandra, who just returned from Jerusalem, to share with us what she has seen.

Alessandra Buzzetti: Thank you. First of all, thank you for the invitation to be here at the New York Encounter. It's my first time. As Riro said, I've been living in Jerusalem for almost five years, and certainly, these last four months have been the most painful and difficult—from a professional but also from a human point of view. It's different to cover a war like this when you've lived in a place for years. You don't just talk about numbers or casualties; a lot of the time, you're talking about friends—friends in both Israel, the West Bank, and Gaza.

At the moment, Jerusalem seems quiet, but it's not really quiet. It feels like a suspended city. Why? Because you can see signs of the conflict in the pictures of Israeli hostages hanging everywhere, and you notice the conflict in many Israelis walking around with rifles. In the Muslim Quarter, it's empty because Muslims under 60 are still forbidden from going to pray at the Al-Aqsa compound. Even the Christian holy places are almost empty — the Church of the Holy Sepulchre is nearly deserted, and so is the Church of Gethsemane.

I go there often, not just because I have friends there who are a great support for me, but because I think it is the place that best reflects what the Holy Land is experiencing right now — the night of Jesus in Gethsemane. Why? Because that's when Jesus appeared in his most radically human form, showing fragility, fear, and anguish, but still surrendering completely to the Father. His words of truth became a testimony understandable to everyone because they were radically human.

The Holy Land is deeply wounded, and it's very difficult for Jews to see the pain of Palestinians, and vice versa. I was struck by the words of Etgar Keret, a well-known Israeli writer and non-religious Jew. I interviewed him for my network, and he talked about "selective empathy." He said we can look at the other side as human beings, but it's difficult. He added, "It gives me comfort to read the words of the Pope, because he is the only one who can express closeness to both sides."

It wasn't a political judgment but an expression of a deeply human need. And in those words, he found the answer. This highlights the mission of Christians in the Holy Land — the smallest community, but the only one that includes members from all the parties involved in the conflict.

Now, just a quick overview: Nearly 10 million people live in the state of Israel, and Christians make up only 1.9%. Among them are Arabs with Israeli passports, illegal immigrants with children born in Israel who speak Hebrew and study in Israeli schools, and even some Jews who have converted to Christianity. Some Christians also serve in the Israeli army. There are 50,000 Christians in the West Bank, where 4 million Muslim Palestinians live, and over 1,000 Christians in Gaza. These figures include Christians of all denominations. The Catholic community, the Latins, is led by Cardinal Pizzaballa.

The violence of this war is also affecting internal relations among Christians, which were already complicated. Now, belonging to the Church is even less automatic. Expressing a desire for reconciliation is incredibly difficult. Forgiveness has long been a taboo in the Holy Land, and today, with the overwhelming suffering and number of innocent victims, it feels even more so.

The Christian community in Gaza is suffering greatly. Most have taken refuge in their parish compound, staying despite repeated evacuation orders from the Israeli army. The displaced in the South also fear a ground military operation. The death toll in Gaza has reached nearly 30,000, including 27 Christians. The last Christian to die was a man who needed dialysis but couldn't receive treatment in the South. He died alone, without his family, just a few weeks ago.

I knew almost all the Christians who have died. I visited Gaza six times before the war. No journalists are allowed to go inside Gaza independently now, only with the Israeli army for a few hours. I haven't gone in yet, but we'll see.

Despite everything, the small Christian community inside Gaza rarely complains. They live under the harsh reality of the Islamic Hamas regime, without freedom. And now they face even more challenges with getting permits from Israeli authorities to leave Gaza and visit family in the West Bank. Gaza is not far from Bethlehem — just 50 kilometers away.

I've reported on the Christian community in Gaza several times, thanks to Fr. Romanelli, who we will hear from shortly. Gaza once had the best schools, run by Christians, and now many of them are destroyed. Sister Nabila, a close friend of mine who ran one of the best schools there, recently said, "It seems that with this systematic destruction, the Israelis want to eliminate even the few signs of beauty that were still in Gaza."

I'd like to conclude by saying that perhaps today, the glow of beauty, though almost invisible, remains in the physical, small presence of the Christian community—a resilient flame of light in the darkness of death and pain. Thank you. [*audience applause*]

Maniscalco: Thank you, Alessandra. The other person in the slide is Deacon George Anton, who took shelter at the parish with his family. George Anton writes the following:

"I decided with my wife and our three girls not to be evacuated for four reasons. First, we wanted to show our love and sacrifice to Jesus Christ by taking responsibility for defending this church and serving Him, as well as serving the Christians in Gaza. Second, we didn't want to leave the church to be destroyed or occupied or used for anything else but prayer and service. Third, we refuse to relive the same tragedy that happened to our grandfathers in 1948, and we refuse to leave our city. And fourth, we will not allow the Christian presence in Gaza to decrease even more. My family is protected by our Lord Jesus, by the Virgin Mary, and by St. Joseph. We accepted this responsibility, knowing how difficult the war is and how complicated it is to provide food and water. But we succeeded with the support of Pope Francis, Patriarch Cardinal Pizzaballa, Mr. Samuel Yousef, and Fr. David from Jerusalem. My family has grown closer, and we've shared our love in different ways. My wife and I explained to our daughters the meaning of being in a war, the consequences, and our responsibilities as Christians toward our Lord, the Church, and the community. They accepted to share this with us until the end. I'm very afraid for my family, but I believe that Jesus will always choose the best for them."

Now let's hear from Fr. Gabriel Romanelli, the Argentinian-born pastor of the Holy Family parish in Gaza, which is the only Catholic Church there.

[*interview video plays*]

Buzzetti: Gabriel Romanelli, you have been the parish priest of the small Catholic community in Gaza City for the past five years. Where were you on October 7?

Fr. Gabriel Romanelli: I was in Bethlehem, waiting for medicine for one of our sisters inside Gaza. After that, it became impossible to return. I tried many ways to get back to my parish, but it wasn't possible.

Buzzetti: How was daily life for the Christian community inside the Gaza Strip before October 7?

Romanelli: It was a wonderful missionary life. The Gaza Strip is not an easy place for anyone, including the small Christian community. But, at the same time, life in the mission was very active. The Gaza Strip is home to 2.3 million people, and among them, this small Christian community. At the start of the war, we had 1,017 Christians, including 135 Catholics – my direct community. This also included sisters and priests from religious communities such as the Missionaries of Charity, who run two homes for disabled children and adults, with 54 people in their care. The Sisters of the Holy Rosary from Jerusalem run the largest private school in Gaza. The religious Family of the Incarnate Word, which I belong to, also lives in Gaza, along with my vicar, Fr. Yousef.

The most important thing for us was to preserve the presence of our Lord in the Eucharist, to keep Christian life alive among the believers, and to give a witness of our faith — especially through charity. We had very strong relationships with our neighbors and many people who, unfortunately, are now suffering in this terrible war. Gaza was already the largest prison in the world, and now the situation is even worse.

On October 7, 1,200 people in Israel were killed, and on the Palestinian side in Gaza, over 25,000 have been killed — 10,000 of them children. Thousands of people are hungry and thirsty. From the start of this war, almost nothing has been allowed to enter. Our community is part of the Palestinian community. The Catholic and Christian communities in Gaza are Palestinian. Our parish compound is in the largest neighborhood in the Gaza Strip. The people and families told us there was nowhere to go, no water, no electricity. So, we opened our doors to receive the Christian community — both Catholic and Orthodox.

Buzzetti: What have been the most painful moments for you?

Romanelli: First of all, the Israeli attack on the Greek Orthodox Church. Hundreds of Christians from the Greek Orthodox community were taking refuge there. The consequences of the bombing were terrible. The building collapsed, killing 18 people and wounding many more. The Israeli army knew that only civilian Christians were in the compound. After this bombing, we received more people from the Orthodox Church, bringing our total to 700. Now, we are 600.

The second painful moment was when a sniper killed one of our parishioners. She was a music teacher. After that, a sniper killed two more women from our Catholic parish. Nahida was a grandmother and the matriarch of the largest Catholic family in Gaza. It is a very hard, very tough situation. At the same time, the faith of our community is very strong. They start each day with the rosary, then the Holy Mass, and engage in different activities. We've started giving lessons on Sundays in the compound since all the schools are closed. Christian schools were the best in the Gaza Strip. We've also tried to assist the Missionaries of Charity in their mission to preserve life. It's not easy, as no one knows when this war will end, but the faith of the people remains strong. They are connected to Jesus through their faith and the reception of the Holy Sacraments. This is what gives life to our community. An especially beautiful moment was the recent First

Communions of eight children. The Christian community knows that Jesus is with them.

Buzzetti: We know that since the beginning of the war, Pope Francis has been calling the parish community in Gaza almost daily. How important is it for them to receive such strong support from the Pope?

Romanelli: It is a wonderful thing because we feel the closeness of the Pope and the Church in such a difficult context. Even just hearing the Pope ask, "How are you today? We are with you, we support you," is incredibly important.

Buzzetti: What are the most important steps we need to take now to find a way out of this?

Romanelli: The most important thing is to stop this war. We must work for peace and justice. We pray for peace for all people—for Israel and for Palestine. We must not forget the victims on both the Palestinian and Israeli sides. We must not forget the millions of Palestinians in Gaza, Jerusalem, and the West Bank—there are around six million of them. We need to find a solution for peace in Palestine, which will also be good for peace in Israel.

[*video ends, audience applause*]

Buzzetti: Fr. Romanelli appeals for a political solution to the conflict, recalling that almost 4 million Palestinians live in the West Bank. For more than three months, checkpoints have been closed by the Israeli army. There is anger and fear. There is also increasing violence from the settlers. More than half a million settlers live in the West Bank, making it impossible to even think of a Palestinian state that is not geographically fragmented. The most violent settlers are attacking Palestinians, taking advantage of the conflict to prevent farmers from working their land and harvesting olives, even around Bethlehem. A farmer told me that his son was killed by settlers simply because he was trying to go to his olive grove. In fact, olive groves belonging to more than one religious community around Bethlehem are under attack from settlers.

In this next short video, I would like to show what Bethlehem is like today and share the experience of my friend Lena. She is a Christian, a mother of three, and a social worker at Caritas Hospital in Bethlehem, a Catholic hospital.

[*video plays*]

Lena: It is so sad. You find pain in every house in Bethlehem. Why? Because many workers cross checkpoints to go to work, and now they can't. Many people — around 95,000 — work in the tourism sector, and the majority of them are Christians. The main source of income for the people in Bethlehem is tourism, so since October, things have been very difficult.

I work in Bethlehem at a pediatric hospital, where I am responsible for the social work department. During the war, many people could not reach the hospital due to the road closures. Chronically ill children couldn't come for treatment, and families were unable to collect their monthly medication. Around 95% of the patients who come to our hospital are Muslims. Even though it's a Catholic hospital, they trust the services we provide. Many of them come from very remote villages, and it's often the first time they meet Christian families. They often express surprise, saying, "So you are Christians — we've never dealt with people like you." Through our attitude and the way we interact with them, they realize that we are different.

My mother and father always told us, "This is your homeland, and this is where you belong," because wherever we go, we will be foreigners. This is what I want for my children as well. I raised them with the belief that this is where they belong. For us as Christians, Bethlehem is important because it's a source of hope — it's where everything started 2,000 years ago. So where else can we go? But to be honest with you, now I'm recalculating. I'm afraid of this feeling. I'm questioning what future there is for this new generation if things remain the same. They are the future of this country, but unfortunately, the opportunities for the youth are so limited. The only weapon we have is prayer. I've learned that during times of crisis, we must keep our faith, and our faith can be strengthened through companionship. So, we gather every now and then to pray together for peace. Jesus died on the cross and defeated death, and now we see so many people dying. But hope does not stop.

Buzzetti: So now we go quickly from Bethlehem to Jerusalem to hear another voice from the Latin Christian community, the smaller one, St. James Vicariate. Eight priests serve in five communities between Jerusalem, Tel Aviv, and Haifa. In the October 7 Hamas attack, some Christians from St. James's Vicariate also died. They were Asian immigrants caring for elderly Jews in the kibbutz. There are at least 20 Christian men serving in the Israeli army, even in Gaza. And now we can listen to Fr. Piotr Zelazko, who is responsible for the St. James Vicariate.

[video plays]

Fr. Piotr Zelazko: We are a very small church community, maybe one thousand people altogether. We speak Hebrew, and our faithful are members of the Israeli society. So, the last months of the war have been very difficult for us. We pray for the hostages, we pray for our kids who are in the army, and we are trying to navigate this situation through our faith. We try to send the message to the entire society that every life matters. Every life is precious. We shouldn't divide people and talk about them as "This is us" and "This is them." Everyone is our brother and sister. It's always a question of how we react and how we pray. I witness this every day — people who pray for peace, people who are deeply wounded, people who feel their country is under attack.

I will give you an example of a young man who was studying in France. The moment he knew his country was under attack, he stopped his studies and returned to Israel to be a paramedic and help in a hospital. This is an example of what we call Christianity: serving your brothers and sisters. This boy is Catholic, and we often speak and pray for peace. He is wounded by the attack on his country, but he is working and praying for peace. We have no choice; we have to speak the Christian language of love, which is also the language of forgiveness. This is something very difficult to imagine right now because, as a part of Israeli society, we feel the pain and shock of October 7th. The pain is still in our hearts. Society is full of the desire for revenge and anger. But as Christians, we need to rise above these feelings and bring the message of reconciliation and forgiveness. We need to think about what will happen after the war.

[*video ends, audience applause*]

Maniscalco: Father David, what can we do? How can we help these seeds of hope?

Fr. David Grenier: Yes, I think that from here in the US, the first thing to do is to remember that we are Christians. What I mean is that we must give more importance to the truth we see in the Gospel than to what we hear on CNN, Fox News, or MSNBC and what they want us to think. Fr. Piotr just said that our religion is the religion of love. So, it's normal, when we see these images and hear these stories, to feel anger, and at times even hatred. But if anger is what remains, if it's what guides our thoughts, actions, or words, it means we are also victims of this conflict, because God is love, and that means we are drifting away from God. He is the only one who can bring a solution to what's going on in the Holy Land right now.

Something we can do as Christians is to remember the three pillars of Lent that we hear about in the Gospel on Ash Wednesday: prayer, almsgiving, and fasting – and to adapt these to the Holy Land. I'll start with fasting. Of course, we can fast literally; it's always good to fight against evil. But we can also remember fasting as Isaiah describes it in chapter 58, which speaks of removing the yoke, the accusing finger, and malicious speech. If we lavish food on the hungry and satisfy the afflicted, then our light shall rise in the darkness, and our gloom will become like midday. The Lord will guide us always, and they shall call us the repairer of the breach, the restorer of ruins.

As Christians, we are called to fast from our biases, to renounce prejudices that are easy to form, and to try to be bridge builders. Why do we have to take sides? This is not a football game or a movie where you root for the good guys to crush the bad guys. We're talking about human lives, all loved by God. Why can't we be both pro-Israeli and pro-Palestinian, wishing the best for both peoples, denouncing the atrocities committed by both sides, and feeling compassion for the suffering on both sides?

When I speak to my Israeli friends, I feel pain for what they are experiencing. When I speak to my Palestinian friends, I feel pain for their suffering. If we want to build bridges between these two peoples, we can't put all the weight on one side because the bridge will collapse. We need balance for the bridge to stand and for there to be a lasting solution.

This brings me to the second pillar: prayer, which is so important. Even if the two peoples don't want to meet, and it's understandable, can I at least make them meet in my heart and in my prayers? Can I ask the Lord for what is best for both peoples, without trying to dictate the solution? God knows better than we do, and He can find a way to make both peoples flourish. As Christians, this is what we are called to do. You might think I'm being idealistic — and I probably am — but first and foremost, I'm a man of faith. I believe God can still perform miracles, and that's what the Holy Land needs right now.

Finally, almsgiving. Christians in the Holy Land are deeply in need. Many work in the pilgrimage industry — in hotels, restaurants, and gift shops that are closed now. They were closed for two years during the pandemic, and people took out loans to feed their families. Just as they were starting to recover, everything has stopped again. Many Christians have left, and many more are thinking of leaving.

Last week, the Custody of the Holy Land met with 500 young men and women from Bethlehem, and the first question they asked was, "Can you give us one good reason to stay?" People are desperate. They come to our parishes asking for help to buy medicine, pay for surgery, and feed their families. They can't afford school tuition for their children. We have 17 schools, and it's more important now than ever to teach Christian values of respect, openness, and love. We also have a music school that brings together Jews, Muslims, and Christians because music is a universal language.

To continue these activities, funds are needed, even for the sanctuaries, which need repairs. Some of these buildings are 1,700 years old and require constant maintenance. You might ask, "Is this really important when people are starving?" But it's more important than ever because of the symbolism of these shrines. The Holy Sepulchre, for example, reminds us that even when things seem desperate, it only took three days for God to turn deep darkness into light, peace, and life for everyone. That's a message people need to remember right now. And maintaining these shrines provides jobs for Christians in construction.

Finally, I invite those who are courageous to go on pilgrimage, even in small groups. It helps people work and gives them hope. It shows them we are near, not just with words, but physically. For a few days or a week, they can think about something other than their suffering. These are just drops in the ocean of hatred flooding the Holy Land, but for the people they touch, they quench their thirst for hope. For them, it makes all the difference. For them, it changes the world. [*audience applause*]

Maniscalco: And now the final step that we take together is listening to and watching this interview that Alessandra put together. It's with Cardinal Pierbattista Pizzaballa, the Patriarch of Jerusalem. He's been a great friend of the Encounter. This is a beautiful, personal, and heartfelt interview. So let's watch it.

[*video plays*]

Buzzetti: Good afternoon, Cardinal Pizzaballa, and thank you for being with us today in Jerusalem. Two weeks after the beginning of the war, you wrote a letter to your diocese. You chose a verse from the Gospel of St. John as a way to navigate the violence and wounds of the conflict: "I have told you this so that you might have peace in me. In the world, you will have tribulation, but take courage; I have conquered the world." You explain that Jesus won the war by loving it on the cross. Four months later, we see thousands of victims, most of them civilians. We see the pile of physical and moral rubble – it looks like an impossible mountain. What does it mean to you, as a believer and as a patriarch, to carry this cross?

Cardinal Pierbattista Pizzaballa: First of all, the cross is not always easy to take and to bear. It's not something you want to choose. I am not among those who are so saintly and devoted that they want to embrace the cross and are looking for it. The cross means following the way of Jesus. First of all, it's about His love, but it's also about solitude and rejection. From a human point of view, Jesus on the cross failed. But as I said, it's also about forgiveness. And you have to live with all these elements together.

What's painful sometimes is that we tend to think that "the others" — the non-Christians, those outside our community — are the source of all these emotions, feelings, and attitudes. But in reality, this cross is everywhere, even within your own community. At the end, Jesus was also abandoned by His apostles and disciples. So you need a strong reference point in your life to remain stable and solid. Love is never just an emotion; love is also an attitude, a conviction. But you need strong elements in your life. As Jesus said on the cross, "Father, into your hands, I commend my spirit." So, this is first of all about your relationship with God, your faith.

It's also important to have friends who help you see the reality you're living in from different perspectives. Otherwise, you risk closing yourself off. This is the danger — to become closed in your sorrow, in your pain, in misunderstanding, and so on. You need to continuously renew this love that keeps you here. You renew it through prayer and through friends, who are like windows that allow you to look beyond the walls of your life. This is how I concretely live through this very painful and difficult situation.

At the same time, we understand that all of this doesn't come from bad intentions but from misunderstandings and fears. As a father — because, in the end, I am the father of this church — I have to understand where all this is coming from. But I must also remain aware that I need to keep giving direction, not surrender to the situation. Giving direction means remaining stable and consistent with what I said: "In this world, you will have tribulation, but I have won the war." If He has won the war, it means there is hope. There is trust that we can remain a place of light and not darkness.

Buzzetti: The war seems to have dimmed the light of Christmas in Bethlehem — no Christmas tree, no decorations in the streets. You made your solemn entrance on Christmas Eve with a small group of people. You were criticized by Palestinians for meeting with Israeli President Herzog, considered an enemy by Palestinians. How do you live your role as a father to all, especially when each party, even within your community, wants exclusive love?

Cardinal Pizzaballa: Even today, after more than a month, two months now, some people are still complaining about that visit. But love cannot be exclusive. If it's exclusive, it cannot be love. Love is always open, always gratuitous. St. Paul says in his first letter to the Corinthians that love is patient, love is kind, and so on. Love cannot be exclusive.

What people sometimes ask for is not out of love, but out of fear — fear of being abandoned, fear of being misunderstood or unsupported. A leader should listen, but also, as I said, provide guidance. It's important to meet with the President of Israel, regardless of his position, because he's the institutional representative of the state. We cannot avoid this. At the same time, it's clear that we are in solidarity with the Palestinian people—that's without question. We express this very clearly through statements, interviews, and in many other ways.

We must remain faithful to the truth, and the highest expression of love is truth. We shouldn't confuse love with emotions. Emotions are prevailing now, and that's understandable. I'm not judging or condemning that. But it's my duty as a pastor to say, "Yes, I have to do this even if you don't like it. Yes, I have to meet the President. Yes, I stand in solidarity with you." To love one doesn't mean to hate the other. That's what people sometimes ask of us, but I cannot accept that — not as a person, not as Pierbattista, and not as a pastor.

Buzzetti: This year, you were unable to make your traditional Christmas visit to the small Christian community in Gaza. They decided not to leave the parish compound, despite repeated evacuation orders from the Israeli army. You have spoken about their witness of interior peace. Could you tell us a little more about that? Are you worried that this small community might disappear from the Strip?

Cardinal Pizzaballa: The risk is there, of course. The living situation in Gaza is absolutely horrible, terrible. I don't even know what other words to use. They have every reason to complain and blame others from a human point of view, but they're not doing that. Every week, I ask them to gather in the church, which is the only big space, and I tell them, "If you want to leave, let us know and we will try to help you." But so far, except for a few, they all say, "We want to remain. We don't know where to go." One of them said, "In this flood, we want to be Noah's Ark," which is a beautiful image.

They have their problems. They are not perfect or saints, but in this terrible situation, they are giving a wonderful testimony of what it means to live the Christian faith.

Buzzetti: In recent months, political leaders have used the Torah and the Quran to justify the elimination of the other side, a story that has been repeated for centuries in the Holy Land. At the beginning of the year, you stated, "Our small Christian community could make the difference in fostering the desire for encounter and freedom in relation to all. It is my dream, it is my madness."

Cardinal Pizzaballa: First of all, we must say that the use of scriptures, the sacred books, to justify violence and war is something we Christians cannot tolerate any longer. We have to be clear about this. I don't understand it, and I think we cannot accept it. One thing missing in this war is the silence, or the absence, of religious leaders. The Pope is speaking, and we Christians, after all, are speaking, but I haven't heard anyone from other religions — I don't want to exaggerate — but at least I haven't heard strong voices from other religious leaders calling for moderation, reconciliation, or for carefully considering the rights and lives of others. Everyone is retreating into their own context, and I think that's a serious problem. After this war, interfaith dialogue cannot be the same. We can't consider this war just a transitional period — something will change. We need to talk about it, we need to raise these points.

Sometimes you feel like a voice in the desert. You feel like you're speaking, but your words aren't touching reality. That's a temptation we face. But I've kept thinking about something over the past months since October, and I consider it very important — something I never considered with this perspective before. It's the beatitude: "Blessed are the meek, for they will inherit the earth" — not heaven, but the earth. In this moment, violence seems to be the force that will determine the destiny of humanity, but that is not the ultimate destiny. The destiny of humanity is built by the meek—those who, day after day, are building their own lives and the lives of others. It's important to remind ourselves of this.

Buzzetti: What response do you expect from your request for a clear and definitive word of truth that will resolve the conflict at its root?

Cardinal Pizzaballa: This is an important point. One aspect of this war, and of wars in general, is the use of language — the way we express things as they are. But we must speak the truth with a perspective that doesn't close doors, but instead speaks the truth with love. If you only speak the truth without love, you can become a destroyer — you back the other person into a corner. But if you say, "I don't understand you; I cannot accept what you're doing, but you are still my brother," you keep the channel open. You can't have dialogue, mediation, or people to talk with if you refuse to acknowledge their existence — their rights, their attitudes, their expectations, and demands. So, the first thing we have to do is to speak the truth, and not just say something, but accept the entire context—their life and our life.

I also think it's important for us — the Church and the Holy See — to do everything we can to help, to support efforts, and to find channels of communication. At the same time, it's clear to me that those responsible for what's happening cannot also be responsible for the reconstruction. One of the problems we face, not only here but especially here, is the need for new leadership.

Buzzetti: The theme of the New York Encounter is "Tearing Open a Sleeping Soul." Have you cried in these last four months?

Cardinal Pizzaballa: I don't like to talk about these things, but of course, I'm human. Yes, there are moments when, in the privacy of your room, you express your emotions before God, asking for help.

Buzzetti: Is it possible that pain can open our hearts and eyes, rather than blind them?

Cardinal Pizzaballa: Pain can open, but pain can also close. It's important to talk and not abandon anyone. It's essential to stay close, because if someone is left alone, pain can lead them to despair. So, it's very important to remain present and keep communication channels open—to always offer a helping hand.

Buzzetti: Do you have a specific message you'd like to communicate to the American people who will listen to you next week?

Cardinal Pizzaballa: What I keep saying is that, first of all, we need their prayers. We need your prayers—I believe in the power of prayer. The other thing we need is this: we don't need to see the same divisions in the United States and elsewhere in the world that we have here. Here, we are divided—Palestinians, Israelis, left, right, inside the Church, outside the Church. We don't need you to imitate our divisions. We need you to help us reconcile, but you have to remain different from us.

[*video ends, audience applause*]

Maniscalco: Speak the truth, but say it with love, because words can either be the voice of hope or the sword of division. Let the three pillars of Lent accompany us. And when it comes to concrete help, yes, financial support is needed. We need money for the New York Encounter, we need money for the Holy Land, and that's one thing we can actually do. We can even turn prayer into a donation. So, as Fr. David requested, we can support the Holy Land through the Good Friday collection, correct?

Fr. Grenier: Yes, on March 29, all the collections taken worldwide in all the churches go to the Holy Land so we can continue our work. So please be generous for the good of the Christians in the Holy Land.

Maniscalco: Thank you. Once again, a round of applause for Fr. David and Alessandra. [*audience applause*]

BEYOND LEFT AND RIGHT

A discussion on the nature, role, and future of the U.S. Supreme Court, with **Stephanos Bibas**, *Judge of the United States Court of Appeals for the Third Circuit, and* **Jeffrey Pojanowski**, *professor of law, Notre Dame University. Moderated by* **Giuliana Carozza Cipollone**, *lawyer and former clerk at the Supreme Court.*

Introduction

In the last few years, and particularly now, the U.S. Supreme Court has often been an object of controversy and has not been spared accusations of being essentially a political tool. Against this background, we would like to be helped to look at it more objectively and understand better its role, nature, decision-making processes, and source of its jurisprudence. Is it possible to rekindle, to use an expression in our theme, a greater trust in this essential institution of American society? Speakers will address these questions.

Giuliana Carozza Cipollone, moderator: Good evening, everyone, and thank you for joining us for this evening's panel on the Supreme Court — its nature, role, and future in our society. My name is Giuliana Carozza Cipollone. I'm a lawyer in Washington, DC, and I spent last year clerking at the Supreme Court. I'm honored to be joined today by our two distinguished guests.

Professor Pojanowski is a professor of law at Notre Dame Law School.

He teaches and writes in the areas of jurisprudence, legal interpretation, and the natural law tradition. Professor Pojanowski previously practiced law in Washington, DC, and clerked for then-Judge, now-Justice John Roberts when he was on the U.S. Court of Appeals for the D.C. Circuit, and for Justice Kennedy on the Supreme Court.

Judge Bibas is a judge on the U.S. Court of Appeals for the Third Circuit. Before his appointment to the bench, Judge Bibas was a professor of law and criminology at the University of Pennsylvania Law School. He has also served as an Assistant U.S. Attorney in the Southern District of New York and as a law clerk to Judge Higginbotham on the Fifth Circuit and to Justice Kennedy on the Supreme Court. Both speakers have more detailed bios on the New York Encounter website.

Since the founding of our country, the Supreme Court has been deeply involved in the political controversies of the day. Most recently, as many of you know, the Court has decided legal questions regarding abortion, the right to own a firearm, affirmative action programs, and major executive actions by the Trump and Biden administrations. Each time the Supreme Court has ruled on such issues, it has sparked extensive political and societal debate about the underlying questions.

For example, last term, the Court was tasked with deciding a discrete question: Are affirmative action programs legally permissible under the Equal Protection Clause of the 14th Amendment, which was proposed by Congress and ratified by state legislatures during Reconstruction? The Court said no, but the commentary that followed engaged with much broader questions. For instance, are affirmative action programs normatively good or bad? What does it mean to live in a truly equitable society? How can and should a country atone for the moral atrocities of its past?

These are all very important questions, but they are beyond the scope of what the Supreme Court actually decided in its opinion, and far beyond what the Court even has the power to decide. The distinction between law and politics — between legal questions and political or moral ones — often gets lost in the public discourse surrounding the Court. But we cannot judge the actions of the Court without first being educated. At the most basic level, we need to be well-informed about what a particular decision did and did not do. More broadly, we need an education about the Court's role in our government system and the limits on its authority. Our speakers are here today to help us answer these questions.

I think it might be helpful to start with some context for what we see today in the discourse around the Court. We often hear that the Supreme Court has never been so politically controversial, so divided, or so comfortable overturning its own precedent. Are these assertions true? Can you comment on the historical context for the political and legal atmosphere we see today? What's actually true, and what is not?

Jeffrey Pojanowski: I think there's an important sense in which a lot of this isn't new, and some of these narratives are not true. Before I sat down to talk, I ran through last year's term – considered a big, controversial term–and the number of cases in which the Supreme Court agreed 9-0 or 7-2, where most justices were in agreement, outnumbered the 5-4 and 6-3 decisions by about two to one. So, mind you, in these cases where there's a lot of agreement, we're talking about some of the hardest cases that come before the Court. Most cases don't get litigated because the law is clear and easy to apply. Very few cases go to final judgment, and fewer still are appealed up to the Supreme Court. So even among these challenging cases, there's still more agreement than disagreement.

With respect to overturning precedent, John Adler, a professor at Case Western Reserve, did a study suggesting that the Roberts Court is actually less likely to overturn precedent than its predecessors. And there's a sense in which judicial controversy isn't new either. Many of us have heard of *Marbury v. Madison* – the case that gives us judicial review, the power of the Supreme Court to say what the law is. The origins of that case were rooted in partisan conflict between President James Madison and Thomas Jefferson over appointments. So, judicial review in the United States arose in the context of heated partisan disagreement, making it an old story.

What I do think is new – and I'll be quiet and let Judge Bibas talk – is that the federal government does a lot more than it used to, for better or worse. As a result, what the federal courts do is more important than it was 50 or 100 years ago. Combine that with a modern news cycle, where people are interested in what's happening at the Court, and you get more fervor and attention than there used to be. This makes the Court seem more prominent and divisive than it used to be.

Stephanos Bibas: First of all, thank you for having us here. I want to second what Professor Pojanowski just said – the Court becomes a lightning rod for controversies, but we have short historical memories. The fights between Federalists and Anti-Federalists over the Louisiana Purchase were a big deal. Our country was even more divided during the Civil War and the Gilded Age, with the debates over laissez-faire capitalism around the turn of the 20th century. There was open fighting between Democrats and Republicans over the role of the government and what the courts should allow or prevent. And of course, there was major controversy during the demise of Jim Crow and the civil rights movement.

So, our society goes through cycles of polarization and tribalism. Now, modern media amplifies this, and the federal government's footprint has grown, making what happens at the federal level more consequential. That seems to me more like a symptom than a cause.

Cipollone: Yes, I absolutely agree. What you both said about short institutional memory is important. If you look back at the role of the courts—not just the Supreme Court but also the Fifth Circuit and district courts during the Civil Rights Movement – they played a critical role in enforcing the laws of that time. We've lost some of that history, and when people point out that the Court today is playing a similar role in political controversies, they often ask, "Why should we let the Court have this power? These are unelected judges with life tenure." It sometimes seems like the justices and other federal judges have too much power, and that's often criticized in the media. How would you respond to that?

Judge Bibas: I think there is widespread confusion about what I do when I decide a case. I try to be very, very careful to say I'm not here to determine if something is good or bad policy. First of all, I'm not allowed to, and no federal judge is allowed to reach out and say, "Hey, this issue in the newspaper looks really interesting. Let me weigh in." I have to wait until someone who is harmed brings a case into court. This is called the "case or controversy" limitation. Sometimes, until someone has been harmed, it can take a long time. For instance, President Biden announced a loan forgiveness program, but until someone was harmed by that program, the courts couldn't opine on it. Eventually, a state agency that lost money because of it brought the case, but many issues never make it to court because no one has been harmed. Such matters have to be hashed out between the President, the House of Representatives, and the Senate.

But even when a case comes to us, we're supposed to exercise restraint. Many issues are meant to be left to state courts. When cases do reach the federal courts, we are supposed to avoid constitutional questions if possible, and we generally do. Our task is to focus on the relief needed for the party in front of us. The side effect may be a broader precedent, as in the Students for Fair Admissions case regarding affirmative action. Even in that case, a lot was left unresolved. For example, is the decision limited to education? What will it mean for employment or housing? Those questions will need to be addressed in future cases.

The reason we focus on real individuals who have been harmed is so we can base our decisions on the facts of each case. This approach may seem unsatisfying, but we are not issuing legislation that applies to everyone in all circumstances. Each case is unique. Often, the headlines suggest that the Court has "blessed" or "cursed" affirmative action, but that's an oversimplification. Worse yet, headlines may say the Supreme Court "upheld" a lower court decision, but what that really means is that the Court declined to review the case. The Supreme Court hears less than 1% of the cases brought to it. When it declines to hear a case, that doesn't imply agreement or disagreement with the lower court's decision — it just means the justices didn't feel the need to intervene.

Professor Pojanowski: I think that's right. The U.S. court system is distinct from other countries' constitutional systems in that we require "standing" — the need for a person to show they have been injured before they can bring a case. Some jurisdictions don't have this requirement; people can go to court just to challenge a government action or ask the court to weigh in on an issue. There are pros and cons to that. If the government is doing something wrong and no one is harmed, they can get away with it. But the benefit of the U.S. system is that the case-or-controversy requirement recognizes that courts are not the only branch responsible for upholding the Constitution. Every officer of the government, from legislators to police officers, has an obligation to follow the Constitution and the law. Courts are not there to declare what the law is in the abstract — they declare what the law is in the context of resolving real disputes.

This also helps mitigate concerns about why courts have so much power. The courts can only act within the limits of a real case or controversy. Of course, if the Constitution or a statute requires a decision, the courts cannot avoid making it. For example, in *Brown v. Board of Education*, the Supreme Court couldn't just avoid ruling because they feared controversy. The Constitution prohibits "separate but equal," and the Court had no choice but to rule for Brown, even if it was going to upset people. That doesn't mean courts should seek out constitutional issues, but when the law requires a decision, courts have to act, regardless of the consequences.

Cipollone: There are also procedural limitations that, while they may not prevent a case from being heard, do tie the court's hands once it's there. For example, statutes of limitations mean that even valid claims must be brought within a certain time. Parties can also waive or forfeit legal arguments, and if they do, the court can't reach those issues, even if a judge or justice believes that argument is the correct one. What are some of these other constraints?

Judge Bibas: There's a whole package of constraints that guide what we're supposed to do. When I became a judge, I took an oath, which the founders took very seriously. This oath pledges to administer justice without respect to persons, to give equal right to the poor and the rich. So when I'm working on a case, I keep that oath in mind. Judges come from diverse backgrounds, but by the time we reach this point in our careers, we've developed a shared legal vocabulary that helps us focus on what the law requires, rather than personal or political views.

This is much less inflammatory than what you might hear from pundits on TV, because we're simply trying to follow what the Constitution says, except where it's been amended, and what the laws say, except where they've been amended. Often, we narrow our opinions to focus on what we need to do to give justice to this particular person, and maybe provide some guidance to lower courts for future cases.

Sometimes, the answer is that it's too late, or a party hasn't been injured, so we avoid ruling on the merits. In those cases, we simply say, "Take the complaint to Congress." There are problems in the system, but they're not usually with how courts process cases – they're about who can act and when.

Pojanowski: When I think about what Judge Bibas was just talking about—cases that never get brought because there's no viable legal argument or no lawyer would take them—the cases that get resolved and never appealed because no lawyer thinks they can win, it's like the legal system's "dark matter." These easily resolvable cases are like the dark matter of the legal system, similar to when you're driving on the highway and marvel at how few accidents happen despite so many cars going 75 miles an hour. It's amazing how much gets settled without fanfare. That's not to say there aren't controversial cases or cases that pose very hard questions, but I think it's important to note how much the law settles most things quietly.

Cipollone: And to clarify, that 1% of cases that make it to the Supreme Court is 1% of those asking the Supreme Court to take their case, not 1% of every appellate decision. That raises a question: statistically, some of those requests are to correct erroneous decisions. I'm sure none of Judge Bibas's decisions fall into this category, but maybe some others do. So, why doesn't the Supreme Court just correct all the wrong decisions? Why not maximize their capacity to get the law as right as possible? Why are they so selective, and what value is served by letting some erroneous decisions stand when they have the time and authority to correct them?

Pojanowski: I remember when I was clerking, one of the jobs we had was looking at petitions for certiorari, the requests for the Supreme Court to review a case, whether it's from the federal courts of appeals or state supreme courts. One of the clerk's jobs is to go through these cert petitions and summarize them for the justice, along with a recommendation. I recall reading some petitions and thinking, "This is wrong; this person should not have lost," or, "There's a good reason they should have won." But often, the Court says, "This is just wrapped up in a particular set of facts," and there's no broader legal issue to resolve. The Court is not in the business of error correction.

That's a hard thing to internalize because we want the courts to do justice. So why not just correct errors? Part of the reason is that while they could do more, the Court also has to focus on resolving broader legal questions. If they spent time correcting individual errors, they wouldn't have the capacity to resolve the bigger disagreements about what the law means. When the Court takes a case, it usually does so because there's a disagreement between circuits, say, the Third Circuit and the Ninth Circuit, over what a statute or the Constitution means. When that happens, the Court steps in to provide uniformity. But if they spent their time correcting individual errors that don't present broader legal questions, they wouldn't have time for that. Plus, many errors are tied up in factual disputes, and the Supreme Court, made up of nine judges, isn't particularly well-suited to review those.

Bibas: I'll put the same point slightly differently. In the Hippocratic Oath, doctors swear to "first, do no harm." That's an important principle, and as a young lawyer, I wanted to change the world. But by the time you become a judge, you understand that, however bad things may be, you could make them worse by sticking your nose in. Sometimes meddling can freeze things in place and make bad law based on it. There are real problems in the lower courts; justice is expensive, and access to it requires a lot of money. Many low-level disputes don't get pursued, or people get out-lawyered by big corporations. But that's not a political problem – it's a problem with the way justice is dispensed in the country, and it doesn't systematically change outcomes at the Supreme Court level.

Cipollone: If I could sum up everything we've discussed so far, the case-or-controversy requirement and other procedural limitations are major ways where legal answers diverge from moral ones. It's also where legal answers diverge from what's often talked about in the media. Another area where this gap comes through is in methods of interpretation. There's a lot of debate about how judges should weigh moral questions when deciding cases. Some argue that judges should apply moral principles, whether their own or society's. Others say morality shouldn't factor into the process at all.

So, my first question is: Is it even possible to make this distinction? Is it really possible to remove your personal lens — your experiences, morals, and unique characteristics — when considering a case?

Bibas: I think the legal system is designed to minimize the impact of those personal factors. We have a common legal training that teaches us to read laws in a certain way. The higher you go in the legal system, the more you rely not just on one judge's opinion, but on a group of judges with collective wisdom. It's like why we use a jury of 12 people — each juror isn't perfect, but together, through deliberation, they produce something reflective of broader societal understanding. The same applies to judges. The back-and-forth with others helps to narrow the focus on the law and reduce the influence of personal preferences.

Another thing is that those who become judges didn't go the politician route. Humility plays a significant role. If I wanted to change the world in a different way, I would have become a politician or a social organizer. But as a judge, my job is to take the materials given to me — the laws — and apply them to the people and facts in front of me. That requires a spirit of humility. It's about interpreting the text of the law: what does the dictionary say? How is this word used in other parts of the law? How does one law relate to another? This process narrows the room for disagreement.

Fifty or sixty years ago, the Supreme Court had a more freewheeling method of interpretation. Chief Justice Warren would start arguments by asking, "Is it right? Is it fair?" But under the influence of Justice Scalia, the Court shifted. As Justice Elena Kagan said, "We're all textualists now." Today, the Court debates the precise meaning of words like "adjacent" versus "adjoining," focusing on what Congress told us. If Congress wants the Clean Water Act to be broader, it should amend the law. This approach is more politically neutral and helps diffuse politically charged interpretations, explaining why there's so much unanimity among judges.

One area where moral considerations might come into play more openly is criminal sentencing. There, a judge has a role in balancing factors like how much the defendant deserves punishment, how sorry they are, and their prospects for reform. But that's a unique situation at the trial level and doesn't play into how we handle appeals.

Pojanowski: The question is, can you separate law from moral judgment?

It's like the old joke about infant baptism: Is it possible? Yes, I've seen it done. Hard cases are hard, and in very tough cases, it may be difficult to separate moral judgment from legal craft, especially when sifting through evidence. A judge might want to work hard to ensure they aren't weighing the evidence in a way that leans toward a preferred outcome. You need to be aware of that tendency.

One of the hardest things for my first-year law students, when I teach them torts, is understanding that while tort law deals with people wronging each other and seeking redress, there are well-established rules that sometimes cut against our moral intuitions. These rules could be bad and may need changing, but what's striking for students is realizing that the law doesn't always align with their personal sense of justice. They learn to operate within this artificial universe of norms – there's precedent, doctrine, and a game being played, and they start to understand the next move.

Imagine you had a relative whose will wasn't clear, and it's unclear whether the bequest would help your kids or go to a cousin you're estranged from. Your job would be to figure out what the will means based on what you know about the person's life. Hard legal interpretation is often like that – deciphering what a statute or phrase meant when it was enacted, as in the 14th Amendment after the Civil War. These become technical legal questions, like determining the difference between "adjacent" and "adjoining" in different statutes.

A certain kind of skeptical lawyer might argue that judges think they're being neutral but are really doing politics and rationalizing it after the fact. But I tend not to believe in arguments from false consciousness because they're impossible to refute. That said, hard cases are indeed hard, and judges can sometimes be swayed by their passions, but it is possible to separate law from personal judgment in many cases.

Cipollone: What you're saying – that the legal system is designed to filter out personal preferences – implies that this is a good thing, which I also believe. But some people, on both the left and the right, argue for a more activist or individualized approach to judging. Why is this more neutral method of judging consistent with the common good?

Bibas: That's a great question. Let's start with the phrase "the common good." Yes, our polity is designed to promote the common good, but the question is whether judges are the ones supposed to aim directly at it, or if they are part of a broader system where, by doing their jobs and staying in their lane, they contribute to the common good.

This ties into different views of human nature. There's a famous legal philosopher who has an optimistic view of judges — he imagines an ideal judge, Hercules, who is supremely strong, smart, and confident, aiming at what's best. But if you believe in human limitations — whether through a concept like Original Sin or just general skepticism about human perfectibility—you might be more cautious about entrusting one person with too much power.

The Founding Fathers had a strong sense of human nature's limits, including selfishness, partisanship, and the need to limit individual power to prevent tyranny. That's why I lean towards the humble approach, like that of the late, great Judge Leonard Hand, who often said, "This law doesn't seem very sensible, but it's my job to apply it, not rewrite it." By not trying to remake society, we avoid the danger of a willful, activist judge creating outcomes that others might see as nightmarish. Unintended consequences can arise when you start twisting the law to fit what seems just in one case, without considering the ripple effects on the broader legal framework.

The principle of "do no harm" is essential. By humbly respecting the role of judges and the laws as written, we ensure a stable, predictable legal system. If we see injustice, maybe it's Congress's job to change the law, but it's better to have consistency rather than an ever-shifting target based on the whims of individual judges.

Pojanowski: I agree with that. We mentioned Justice Scalia earlier, and when the conservative legal movement responded to the Warren Court's activism in the '60s and '70s, there was a tendency to overcorrect. They reacted by saying, "We don't want to care about moral questions at all. Let's just do law, no morality." But that approach ignored the fact that law and morality are intertwined.

I think there's been a shift back towards recognizing that, even when you're working within technical legal doctrine — whether it's interpreting a statute's original meaning or following precedent – you're doing it for moral reasons. A reasonably just legal system promotes the common good, and by staying in your lane, you are contributing to that good. You may have to make decisions that aren't what you personally would have chosen, but you're doing it for moral reasons, like maintaining the rule of law and respecting the Constitution.

Even when you hand down a judgment that isn't your personal preference, you're refusing to make a moral judgment for good moral reasons. So while you can't completely separate law from morality, especially when choosing a method of interpretation, it's often moral reasoning that tells you, "This is not my job; this is someone else's role." By faithfully applying the law as it was intended, you're serving the common good.

Pojanowski: You are promoting the common good by staying in your lane, by trying to identify what the law is. You may have to sometimes bite the bullet and hand down judgments that you think are not what you would have done – not something wicked, we're not talking Nuremberg laws, but just something you wouldn't personally agree with. But even when you hand down a judgment that's not what you would have done, whether because of precedent, statutes, or your understanding of the Constitution, you're staying your hand and refusing to make a moral judgment for very good moral reasons.

Ultimately, you can't completely separate law from morality, especially when you're choosing a method of interpreting the Constitution or statutes. There's no avoiding morality at the higher level of asking, "How should I interpret?" and "What is my role?" But it may be that natural law or moral reasoning tells you, "This is not my job – it's someone else's job." In that case, you need to be faithful to what you think the Constitution meant at that particular time, and you're doing that for good moral reasons.

Cipollone: Professor, I'm curious – based on your work in the natural law tradition and jurisprudence—can you comment more on what the Church has to say about this, if anything?

Pojanowski: What does the Church have to say about that? Well, I don't have an encyclical at hand, so I'll fall back on Aquinas. Aquinas says that law is an ordinance of reason for the common good, promulgated by a person in authority with care for the community. It's easy to emphasize reason and the common good — law exists to serve the common good, which is, to some extent, knowable by reason. But reason under-determines the common good. There are many wrong ways to order a society, but there are also a wide range of morally acceptable ones.

The question then becomes: who has authority? If it's the legislature or the framers of the Constitution, they've hopefully made a reasonable, moral decision about the form of order and law. The job of the interpreter is to figure out what that ordinance of reason was and respect that authority. We need authority and reasonably just legal rules to cooperate and coordinate. There's also a moral element in respecting what the polity has judged before us — 225 years ago, a supermajority decided how we're going to live together until we change it accordingly. In a reasonably just polity, we have a moral obligation to adhere to that law.

People often complain about being ruled by the "dead hand of the past," but without rules to cooperate, coordinate, and define our rights and obligations, we'd have chaos. Again, this assumes a reasonably just legal order. You could be an originalist in North Korea, but I wouldn't recommend it as a judge.

Lastly, natural law tells you that if you have a deeply unjust law and don't have the jurisdiction to change it, you may have a moral obligation not to enforce it. You may need to resign, recuse yourself, or not enter judgment. However, it's a violation of natural law to lie about what the law is. You cannot take authority you don't have. To do so would violate natural law and offend the common good. So while you may need to step aside, you cannot say the law is something it's not, because that in itself would violate the common good.

Cipollone: That's all really helpful in understanding how theories of judicial minimalism are not inconsistent with the common good. It's not an abdication of your moral obligation, but rather a posture of humility. It recognizes that our entire governmental system works to promote the common good, and you, as a judge, play a small part in that. Your fidelity to that role is what makes the whole system function.

Bibas: Can I just add to that? I'm no expert on natural law, and I'm not Catholic, but I'm a big fan of *A Man for All Seasons*. You know, "all of England is planted thickly with the trees of the law, and what would happen if you cut down all these laws? And then the devil turned on you? Where would you be?" I think people who are so eager to instrumentalize or twist the law towards certain ends forget what someone with bad intentions could do in a land without that kind of structuring decision-making. I see a lot of youthful myopia, with optimism about, "If I were a dictator, I'd do this," but very little recognition of what someone whose vision of the common good differs from yours could do if we bypassed these laws.

Cipollone: We've talked a little about how our judicial system is misunderstood and the controversies surrounding it. What are reasons for hope? Where do you see all of this going? And what can we do — whether as lawyers, judges, professors, or non-lawyers — to cultivate that hope?

Pojanowski: I wish I were more optimistic. But I think events like this are fantastic, and being a good, informed citizen — rather than just reading clickbait — can help. There are some good, unbiased resources for those interested in the Supreme Court. SCOTUSblog is a pretty good, nonpartisan explainer of what's going on with the Court. There's also a podcast called *Divided Argument* with Will Baude and Dan Epps, who are sort of center-left and center-right, and they discuss the Court in a balanced way. So, becoming an informed citizen is helpful.

I don't think things are going to calm down anytime soon, and I'm not sure the Court can do much about that. We live in a time of constant news cycle outrage. My hope is long-term. I think, for many people, following news and politics — especially when it comes to the Court — has replaced community and religion as a source of meaning. Tocqueville said Americans have always been law-obsessed people, but back then, we had meaningful local government, strong civic institutions, and healthy faith communities that helped counterbalance the centrifugal forces of politics.

Long-term cultural solutions are hard to prescribe, but I think caring less about the Court and focusing more on rebuilding communities would be a first step. However, I'm not sure that's coming anytime soon. So, sorry for being so pessimistic.

Bibas: I'm pessimistic too, but in terms of what you can do, our system of government was built around in-person deliberation. If you look at the Bill of Rights, about half of it is about the jury — the quintessential face-to-face deliberation with people from your community. People often complain about jury service before they do it, but afterward, they usually say, "Hey, that was pretty amazing!" They come away with a new respect for the law and how seriously it's taken.

If you want to understand the legal system, do less following of the national media and do more hands-on involvement. Serve on a jury, watch a trial — most trials are public. You can go watch a Supreme Court session in person. Listening to oral arguments is good, but being there in person gives you a real sense of the focus and legal precision. Wherever you live, watch your local courts, attend city council meetings. The more you get out of the virtual space, the more you get off your phone and out of this cartoonish view of your fellow citizens, the healthier you'll be. Unfortunately, it's a countercultural thing, but it's a good rule for life.

Cipollone: Thank you. Unfortunately, our time is coming to a close, but I think that's a great place to end—on the need for real encounter. [*audience applause*]

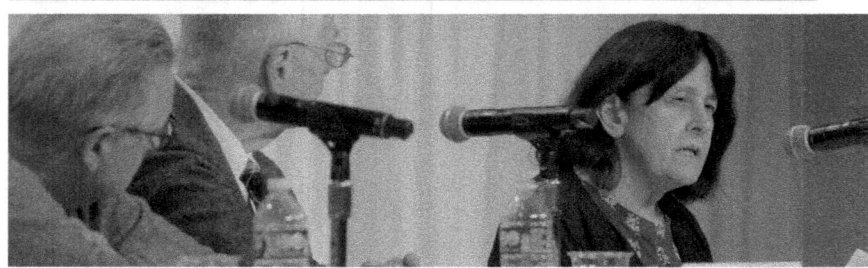

From Death Into Life

Stories of forgiveness and hope, with **Gilbert King**, *journalist, and* **Rachel Muha**, *founder of the Brian Muha Foundation, with concluding remarks by* **John McCarthy**, *dean of the School of Philosophy, Catholic University of America.*

Introduction

One of the Encounter's aims this year is to explore how our humanity—even when it is asleep—can always be reawakened. Encountering a mother who went through the unspeakable suffering of having a son murdered by gang members and who not only forgave the killers but also created initiatives to "show inner-city young people that they are loved and have an opportunity of a bright future" is definitively one of those events that may "rekindle our soul" and provide reasons for hope. Or, getting to know the story of an innocent man who spent 35 years in prison and forgave the person who actually committed the murder for which he was unjustly incarcerated provides an opportunity for our humanity to be reawakened. On this note, on hope and its reasonable foundation, we will end our weekend and continue our journey.

John McCarthy, moderator: Welcome to this final encounter of this weekend of encounters. My name and affiliation are in the program. On the night of February 24, 1987, Leo Schofield received a call from his wife, Michelle. She had finished her shift at a local restaurant and said she would see him soon. Instead, she was brutally killed. She was only 18. Shortly thereafter, Leo, three years her senior, was arrested for her murder by an overly aggressive prosecutor. Despite shoddy police work and an appallingly weak case, Leo was convicted, thanks to a witness with a penchant for lying, a feckless defense attorney, and the deliberate suppression of evidence. Leo has spent the last 36 years in prison, lost an appeal to have his case reheard, and has been denied parole twice, despite having an almost immaculate prison record. Astonishingly, he has forgiven the man who has admitted to many people that he murdered Michelle. Leo has even expressed a readiness to forgive the prosecutor who, despite all the evidence to the contrary, unreasonably insists on Leo's guilt.

Just after noon on May 31, 1997, Rachel Muha received a phone call that no mother should ever receive. Her second son, Brian, had been abducted at gunpoint along with his housemate, Aaron Land. Both were 18, as were the two young men who beat, robbed, and shot them dead. The killers were subsequently convicted of murder and sentenced to life in prison without the possibility of parole. Rachel, I am again astonished to report, forgave the two men who killed her son, and she did so even before the police located his body. Her eldest son, Chris, quickly joined her in this extremely painful and endlessly ongoing act of forgiveness.

On my right is Gilbert King, a Pulitzer Prize-winning author who has spent much of the last four years of his life uncovering what has proven to be massive evidence of Leo Schofield's innocence. Together with Kelsey Decker, he has documented his findings in a gripping podcast entitled *Bone Valley*, which I urge every one of you to download and listen to. Gilbert's passion for justice is apparent in that podcast, in the three books he has published, and in pieces he has written for *The New York Times*, *The Washington Post*, and *The Atlantic*. I am honored to sit in his company.

I am also honored, or rather humbled, to be seated next to Rachel Muha. Long before the brutal murder of her son, Rachel was a vibrant participant in the charitable activities of her parish in Columbus, Ohio. After Brian's death, she poured her heart into works of Christian mercy. Initially, the Brian Muha Foundation, which she helped found and now runs, provided school scholarships to the most neglected children in Columbus. It then launched an after-school program, a food pantry, an appliance distribution network, and a small farm to give kids a taste of life off the streets. In 2020, she started a school of her own. All of this is the fruit of Rachel's decision to forgive. All of it aims to help young people know the love of God and neighbor, and to grow in their own love of neighbor and God.

We will first hear from Gilbert.

Gilbert King: Thank you. Thanks, John, that was really lovely. And I just want to say thank you for having me. I'm really honored to be here. This is my first time at New York Encounter, and I can't believe how beautifully it's run and how incredible the lectures and panels I've seen have been. I'm truly honored to be here, so thank you.

I'm going to start with a slideshow to walk you through this story and talk about some of the things John just mentioned.

I'll start by telling you how I got interested in this case. I had written a book called *Devil in the Grove*, which received a lot of acclaim. As a result, I was invited to judicial conferences all over the country. At one such event in Florida, after giving a talk about Thurgood Marshall taking on a case in Florida back in the 1940s, I was signing books when a judge came up to me and dropped a card on my desk. I looked at it and thought, What is this? He simply motioned for me to call him if I wanted to talk.

That evening, I went to dinner with some public defenders and mentioned the judge's card. I asked, What do you make of this? They were puzzled, asking, Is he a sitting judge? He's not supposed to be doing these things. Finally, one of the defenders from the county where this case took place 30-something years ago looked at me and said, I know this case. You should call him. So when I got back to Brooklyn, that's what I did. I called him up and said, Hey, I just wanted to follow up. You left a card at my talk.

The judge then told me the story of Leo Schofield, a man who had been railroaded for a murder he did not commit. He said, I can tell you exactly how it was done. Somebody needs to do this story. I told him I was working on a new book and it would be a while before I could get to it, but to tell me more. I could feel his disappointment as he stressed, This is urgent. I'm talking about a man who's been falsely convicted and is still in prison. I hesitated, but he asked me to do him one favor: Just read the trial transcript.

So I did. I'm not a lawyer, but even I could see something was very wrong with this trial. I had a lot of questions.

So, I got back to him and started asking questions. Basically, he told me about Leo's life. He said that in 1987, Leo had been married for only about six months. Here he is with his wife, Michelle. They borrowed some tuxedos, got married in a church, and were trying to build a life together in a trailer park. Leo was a rock and roll guitarist, and Michelle had just gotten a job as a waitress at Tom's Restaurant. On February 24, 1987, after finishing her shift, she went home, did a bit of laundry, and called Leo from a payphone right across the street from the restaurant. She said, "I'll be right over there in about 10 or 15 minutes." But she never showed up. Hours went by. Days went by. No sign of Michelle. Missing person posters started going out.

Two days after she went missing, they found her car on the side of the Interstate 4 between Orlando and Tampa. Leo rushed to the scene — he's the one in the blue shirt [*points to the screen behind him*] — but there was still no sign of Michelle. He was frantic. He hadn't slept in two days.

The next day, they conducted a helicopter search, tracing the area where the car was found and the last place she was seen — at the restaurant. They found her body in a nearby canal, not far from I-4. She had been stabbed 26 times and left in the canal. This is Leo after learning that his missing wife had been found. He's clearly a broken man, punching the ground, the trees, screaming. It was obviously the most traumatic moment of his life.

Sadly, there were no real leads. No evidence to go on. The case stalled for a long time—about two years—before it finally went to trial. You can see Michelle was this dynamic young woman who had her whole life ahead of her, and then she suddenly went missing. It was a mystery: How did she die?

After about two years, with little evidence, Leo — who had been as cooperative as possible — became the prime suspect. They found a neighbor who claimed she saw Leo carrying something heavy out of his trailer that night and putting it in his car. Based on that eyewitness testimony, they believed they had enough to move forward and charge Leo with the murder, even though there was no physical evidence tying him to the crime scene. He had a pretty solid alibi — he was with his band and friends—and there was only a very limited time during which he could have committed the crime. None of his behavior suggested guilt.

One major issue in the case was that Leo's father was the one who found Michelle's body. Family and friends had been searching the area since the police hadn't committed much to the search. When his father found the body, he told the police, "God led me to her body." This raised great suspicion around Leo's father and allowed the prosecutor to build a theory that father and son were in on it together. The idea was that the father knew where the body was because he had put it there. This theory became the heart of the prosecutor's case, even though there was no real evidence.

A striking point in this case is that the neighbor's testimony about seeing Leo carrying a body made the trailer the alleged crime scene. She also claimed to have heard a vicious argument. However, not a single drop of blood was found in the trailer — nothing. You would think that would be a problem for the prosecutor, but no. He built a circumstantial case and found an explanation for everything.

This is the prosecutor, John Aguero. One of the most disturbing aspects of this case is that all the best evidence against Leo came from Aguero's office — no recordings, no police witnesses, just Aguero's word. Facts became irrelevant. This becomes important later because, at one point, after Leo was arrested and in jail, guess who comes to visit him? John Aguero. Leo had a defense lawyer, but Aguero showed up unannounced. Leo didn't know any better, so he went to meet with him. Leo thought, "Anyone in a suit must have authority; I should cooperate," which he had been doing all along. Aguero told Leo, "I know you didn't kill Michelle. It was your father. If you flip on him now, you'll have total immunity."

Leo's response? "If my father killed my wife, you wouldn't have to offer me immunity. I'd stand up and testify against him. I don't need immunity for that." He said, "I can't take that deal because neither of us killed Michelle." That was the end of the deal. Leo's chance at freedom was gone, but he said that was okay because he knew the truth and wouldn't dishonor his dead wife by admitting to something false.

Ultimately, Leo was convicted of the murder. Miraculously, he didn't get the death penalty. We tracked down one of the jurors, one of the only living jurors from the trial. She told us she didn't think Leo was guilty, but she went along with the others because she felt they were the adults in the room, while she was only 22 years old at the time. However, when it came to the death penalty, she stood firm, saying, "I'm not doing it." She believed the other jurors felt sorry for her or respected her conviction, and they changed their vote to life in prison to appease her. That 22-year-old juror may be the only reason Leo Schofield is alive today. She managed to sway the jury during the sentencing portion of the trial.

Something else happened after Leo had been in prison for about seven years. He met a social worker named Chrissy, who was teaching a life skills class at the prison. Believe it or not, they fell in love. This wasn't a "Ted Bundy groupie" situation. Chrissy was college-educated, with a degree in social work. Leo was an intelligent man, and they genuinely fell in love. It caused some complications – Chrissy had to transfer to a different prison – but she became obsessed with Leo's case and began investigating it on her own. She was particularly puzzled by the fact that there were fingerprints found in Michelle's car that had never been identified. The prints didn't match Leo, Michelle, or anyone who should have had access to the car. They were from a stranger.

Chrissy decided she had to find out who those fingerprints belonged to. She had a friend who was a cop in a nearby town, and she persuaded him to run the prints. Seventeen years after Michelle Schofield's murder, those prints came back as a match to a known killer. This man lived about a mile away from Leo and Michelle at the time. He was already serving time in prison for another murder, and we believe he committed four murders in total, getting away with three of them. The fourth one got him sentenced to life in prison. His name is Jeremy Scott, and his fingerprints were found in the car where Michelle was last seen.

I won't go into too much detail about Jeremy Scott, but he was an extraordinarily violent young man. By the age of 11, he was already being convicted of felonies. He was living on the streets, in and out of foster homes and juvenile detention systems. At age 15, he went to trial for his first murder, but was acquitted and returned to the streets. That's where he crossed paths with Michelle on that fateful night.

Years later, after initially denying any involvement, Jeremy finally confessed to killing Michelle. He began providing details about how it happened. He said he saw her at the phone booth outside the gas station, across from the restaurant where she worked. After she got off the phone, she asked if he needed to use it, but he said no and asked for a ride instead. Michelle recognized him, even though he didn't recognize her – he wasn't good with faces – but she remembered him from the neighborhood and agreed to give him a ride.

That was Jeremy's confession. However, when it went to court, one judge decided Jeremy had no credibility because he had already lied about not being involved, so he couldn't be trusted. As a result, Leo didn't get a new trial. This would happen again and again in Leo's story.

Jeremy also had a girlfriend at the time, and she said they used to frequent the area where Michelle's body was found – it was his secret spot, where they would hang out. He knew the place well. We investigated this thoroughly. Later, we interviewed Jeremy in prison. We only had about an hour and a half with him, but something struck me. One of the pieces of evidence found at the crime scene was a pack of cigarettes, which the police photographed but never collected as evidence. We asked Jeremy what brand he smoked – this wasn't public information because it had never been part of the case. Jeremy said he smoked Marlboros. He went on to describe how, after he killed Michelle, he smoked a cigarette, dragged her into the water, and stole her car.

Everything Jeremy told us matched details he couldn't have known unless he was the killer. In fact, while we were interviewing him, he confessed to another unsolved murder. I'm still working on that case because I can't get law enforcement or the state attorney to take these confessions seriously. Jeremy Scott has essentially confessed to multiple murders, and no one will believe him. It's like he's the luckiest criminal in Florida.

The prosecutor I mentioned earlier – the one who offered Leo immunity

— did something pretty shocking. When he discovered that the fingerprints found in Michelle's car belonged to Jeremy Scott (keep in mind, this same prosecutor had previously prosecuted Jeremy for the murder that sent him to prison), he had a chance to do the right thing. But instead, he brought Jeremy into his office — no police, no tape recorder, no witnesses — and told him to stick to his story that he had only been stealing stereos. In exchange, he promised to help Jeremy with parole. Jeremy, who has a low IQ, agreed, but the promised help never came.

I want to show you Leo today [*points to the screen*]. He's now a grandfather. He and his wife, Chrissy, adopted a daughter, and now they have two grandchildren. They've been married for 30 years. When you think about what kind of marriage that is — these two people have been together through everything. Here's Leo during a recent visit with his family.

After the podcast was released, the narrative around Leo's case began to change. People in the prison started to believe he was innocent. Letters started pouring in. One of the people moved by his story was the tall man in the white shirt on the screen. He's a state senator from Florida and the chair of the Criminal Justice Committee. He's 100% convinced that Leo is an innocent man, and he even testified on Leo's behalf during a parole hearing.

The most remarkable thing about Leo, which comes through in the podcast, is this: How do you survive 36 years in prison when you could've been out decades ago? He had the opportunity to walk free twice if he had just lied, but he refused. When we let him hear Jeremy's confession, it moved him deeply. He was at a point where he was praying for Jeremy. He told us that he had never had the chance to properly grieve for his wife because he had spent all this time defending his own life. He said, "The only way I can get rid of the anger and bitterness is to pray for Jeremy Scott, to forgive him." Leo believes that was his only path to salvation.

Remarkably, Jeremy Scott now believes that helping Leo go free is the one good thing he can do with his life. In one of his recent letters to me, Jeremy wrote, "Mr. King, I just hope the day comes when I can sit in a room with Leo, tell him I'm sorry for what I did to his wife, and ask for his forgiveness." I spoke to Leo about this, and now that he's finally

From Death Into Life

been granted parole, they are planning to meet. Leo is going to be allowed to return to the prison as part of a re-entry program. He's not doing this meeting for himself – he genuinely cares about Jeremy Scott's soul and believes he is worthy of forgiveness.

I believe this story is going to end with Leo's exoneration. He has powerful people advocating for him. Thank you. [*audience applause*]

Rachel Muha: This morning, in the video we saw, Fr. Giussani asked, "Jesus Christ, yes or no?" That is what this talk is about. Good evening, everyone. Thank you for inviting me to speak to you tonight.

St. John Chrysostom said, "The cause of all evil lies in the fact that we consider as alien all things that concern our own body," meaning the Mystical Body of Christ. He said no one is fulfilling his duty if he ignores his neighbor's salvation. In other words, if we love God and remember that every soul is precious to Him, then we can be filled with hope, and we can be merciful. And it's mercy that performs miracles and changes hearts. So I'm glad to come and speak to you tonight about these very things by telling you a story.

I have two sons, Chris and Brian, and they are only 19 months apart. They grew up doing everything together and were best friends. So when it came time for Chris to go away to college, that was a hard year for Brian because Chris chose a college two and a half hours away from us, at Franciscan University. Chris was so happy there that Brian followed him the next year.

The consecration to Jesus through Mary is a very important event at Franciscan University. Chris consecrated himself his first year there on December 8, the Feast of the Immaculate Conception. Brian wanted to do the same when he got there. But Brian was a private person when it came to prayer – he preferred to pray alone, except, of course, at Mass. So he told Chris that he was uncomfortable praying in a group. In response, Chris went to Brian's dorm room every evening for a month, and the boys prayed together. On March 25, the Feast of the Annunciation, Brian consecrated himself to Jesus through Mary.

The Annunciation – the most earth-shattering, life-changing, spectacular event to have ever occurred. God becomes man, and a little, unknown teenage girl stands at the center of it all, says "yes," and changes the world. Changes us. Mary said "yes" no matter the circumstances, no matter the ridicule. She said "yes" to a mystery too great to understand, "yes" to the unknown. And it took even more courage to say "yes" to the known. Mary knew what was prophesied about the Messiah. She said "yes" to the suffering, "yes" to giving us the Savior, "yes" to standing against the attacks of evil, and "yes" to loving those who killed her Son — and that's us. It's our sins that killed her Son. What a mother's heart, born from her love of God. We must want to love like that. How can we refuse to love those who hurt us and those who hurt our children?

So Brian said "yes" on the Feast of the Annunciation, and the next great feast day of the Blessed Mother would become a very important day in Brian's life, and in all of ours.

On May 4, after Brian's first year and Chris's second year at Franciscan, the boys came home. Both decided to study that summer — Chris at Ohio State and Brian back at Franciscan, where the summer courses lasted only five weeks. On May 30, when it was time for Brian to return to Franciscan, we kissed him, hugged him goodbye, and walked with him to the garage. He got into the Blazer, pulled out of the driveway, and waved at us with that great smile of his. Then he drove off, and that was the last time we ever saw Brian.

But I did talk to him one more time. He called when he got to Steubenville to let me know he had arrived safely. He was excited because he was going to live off-campus with two friends, Aaron and Andrew. He told me Aaron was helping him unload the Blazer. I said, "That's good, honey. I'll talk to you tomorrow." He said, "Okay, Mom." I said, "I love you, Bri." He said, "I love you too, Mom," and he hung up. Neither of us knew it, but he had less than 12 hours to live.

Well, the next day was Memorial Day, and it was also the Feast of the Visitation. That morning, flowers were delivered to me. They were from Brian — white roses with just a little hint of pink around the edges. The card read, "Just wanted to say hello, even though I'm away. Love, Bri." So I called Brian to thank him, but Andrew answered the phone. He told me Brian wasn't there and asked for our phone number. Afterward, I hung up and said to Chris, "I think I woke Andrew up because he asked for our phone number as if Brian wouldn't know it." But I learned later that Andrew was being told what to say.

The day went on, and around 2:15 that afternoon, the phone rang. I thought it would be Brian, but instead, it was a voice I had never heard before, and one I will never forget. The person said, "Mrs. Muha, this is Detective Lawless of the Steubenville police. Your son Brian is missing." Darkness fell on that beautiful spring afternoon. I now call that the first worst moment of my life because so many more were to come. But it was also a moment of grace — just a split second where you have to decide: How am I going to face this—with God or without Him? I know that what you decide in that moment makes a huge difference in how you can handle what is to come.

After asking lots of questions and getting no answers, I hung up the phone and said to Christopher, "What are we going to do?" I thank God for Chris, who said, "Let's pray, Mom." That's how we should approach every problem, isn't it? Prayer first, then action.

Detective Lawless said I had to stay home because if Brian could get to a phone, that's where he would call. At the time, we had two phone lines in the house — this was right before cell phones became common — and I knew which line Brian would use if he could. So we used the other one to call everyone we could think of: everyone who knew Brian and Aaron. We asked them, "Have you seen them? Have you heard from them? Do you know where they might be? Who else can we call?" But nobody knew anything.

Family and friends drove from Cleveland, Columbus, New York, Florida, and all places in between to Steubenville, Ohio, to search for two college boys who were missing. One evil act spreads its horror — so many innocent people's lives were forever changed. Chris made a flyer with his brother's picture and information on it, and he went to a copy store to have hundreds printed. When the clerk saw the flyer and Chris's pain, he wouldn't take any money for the printing. He told Chris, "I will pray that Brian is found." Chris walked out of that copy store feeling a little less lonely. One compassionate act spreads its comfort.

Late Tuesday, Detective Lawless said I could go to Steubenville because by then they had two suspects in jail who weren't talking. Their names were Terrell Yarborough and Nathan Herring. The detectives said to them, "There are hundreds of searchers out there looking for the boys — where are they?" Then they added, "The mothers are here. Their hearts are broken. They just want their sons back. Where are they?" Four times Terrell and Nathan lied to us. Four times they said, "Go look here" or "Go look there," and we would all go search, but we never found the boys.

We spent a week in a type of hell. Hell itself is a state of being totally devoid of love — a compulsive, never-ending search for love while knowing, not just wondering, but knowing that love will never be found. It is searching for something you have no hope of finding, but you can't stop searching. How awful. Hell is painful because life without love is the worst pain ever.

We were in a type of hell because we were searching for a particular love — Brian — and we couldn't find him. But at least we were surrounded by others who cared and were searching with us. So we searched. We called Brian's name. We pleaded with people. We knocked on every door. We looked in abandoned buildings, along roadsides, and in dumpsters — afraid of what we might find, but so hopeful that we would find the boys alive. And while we searched, we prayed.

I recently read a quote by Pope Benedict XVI that fit this terrible moment in our lives. He said, "When faced with evil, we often have the sensation that we can do nothing. But our prayers are, in fact, the first and most effective response we can give. They strengthen our daily commitment to goodness." The prayer in my mind all the time was the Our Father. When I reached the words "forgive us our trespasses, as we forgive those who trespass against us," I thought, "Do I really mean that? Can I really pray that?" What is this forgiveness that God wants from us?

I know this: to forgive someone does not mean to excuse them. It doesn't mean you're saying what they did is okay or that they can go on their way. It doesn't mean there should be no punishment, and it doesn't take away their guilt — only God can do that. So what is the Christian meaning of forgiveness? What is it that God is commanding us to do?

I think Christian forgiveness means refusing to harbor any ill will toward someone who has hurt you — refusing to hold on to hatred, bitterness, anger, or thoughts of revenge. And because we are Christians, we must have goodwill toward that person. Forgiveness and its accompanying goodwill are actions, not feelings. We may never feel like forgiving, but that doesn't matter.

Our Lord was asked, "How many times should we forgive?" And in effect, He answered, "Always." Always, with no conditions. He didn't say, "Wait until you feel like it." So we forgive quickly, readily, and especially when we don't feel like it.

To have goodwill toward someone means to be willing to do what is best for that person, and what is best for all of us — to get to heaven. So we must do what we can to help that person get to heaven. God asks a lot of us, but that's the best decision you can make in life: doing God's will.

On Thursday night, we had searched all day long. We were exhausted, and in the chapel on campus, we prayed. I stood up to thank everyone who had been searching with us, knowing they would stay with us as long as it took, and I said out loud, "I forgive these men." God gave me a great gift — one He will give to anyone who forgives without reservation, who forgives when they don't feel like it, even when it involves great pain and struggle. He gave me what I can only call a piece of heaven. It was a calmness, a confidence, and a comfort in the midst of great suffering.

God does not take away our pain because suffering can be valuable and redemptive — after all, our Lord died on the cross. My heart was broken into a thousand pieces, and I think it always will be. But my spirit was never broken, because our God is mighty, and He keeps us whole. All we have to do is lean on Him.

An act of forgiveness allows God to take away what is destructive — anger, bitterness, and revenge — and leave behind what is constructive. And He also gave me, at that time, what I now call a gift in reserve — something I didn't know I had received yet.

On Friday, we had searched all day long, broken up into small search parties. By the end of the day, the group I was with went to the police station to see if they had heard anything. When we arrived, there was no one else there because everyone was out searching. We sat down in a small waiting room for a minute, and then young Officer Anderson walked in. He came over to us and said, "Mrs. Muha, we've been looking for you. We just got word. They found Brian." I asked, "He's alive?" And he said, "No." Then he stood up, backed away, and started to cry.

I had to look at everyone else's faces in the room to see if I had heard what I didn't want to hear. And then I heard the most heart-wrenching sound I've ever heard: Christopher, sobbing. I turned to him and held him. And I learned something that day: when you're down, really suffering, and at your lowest, the devil attacks you. He kicks you when you're down. I felt evil so close to me, and I was tempted to hate those men—the criminals who took, hurt, and killed Brian, and broke Chris's heart. But I thought, "No, I won't hate. I won't hate. If I hate, what will that do to Christopher?" A mother has some influence on her children.

Then I thought, the devil didn't get a victory that early morning of May 31, 1999. I knew how Brian lived his life. He was walking with God, not away from Him. So, the devil didn't get Brian. And he wasn't going to get me, or Chris, or anyone — at least not if we had anything to do about it. Much later, I wondered, "How did I think that clearly in the worst, most painful moment of my life?" That's the gift in reserve I mentioned earlier.

You know how it is when you're angry or upset and you might say or do something that you later have to apologize for? We usually say, "I didn't mean it, I shouldn't have said that, I wasn't thinking straight." But in that act of forgiveness, God was able to take away all the anger and bitterness and leave me with calmness and clear thinking. That's what allowed me to think so clearly in such a terrible, horrible, painful moment. And that's the end of the Our Father, isn't it? "Forgive us our trespasses, as we forgive those who trespass against us. And lead us not into temptation, but deliver us from evil." That's exactly what God does.

When we were told what happened to Brian that early morning of May 31, I also realized that Jesus and Mary had gone into the hill country — this time in Pennsylvania — and taken Brian home. As we learned the horrible details, all I could think was, "How can human beings be so cruel to other human beings?"

The day after Brian was found, I wanted to climb the hill that Brian had climbed and see the place where he met our Lord. If you climb up the hill on Route 22 in Pennsylvania, you'll come to a rosebush. Brian and Aaron were found beneath that rosebush. It came over them like a canopy. It was in full bloom, with white roses tinged with just a little hint of pink around the edges. I take that as a sign from my Blessed Mother, telling me that Brian is okay.

One of Chris's friends pulled a branch from that special rosebush with his bare hands – thorns and all – and gave it to us. We planted it in our backyard, and it took root. It blooms every May. The first week of June, the week Brian was found and buried, it stops blooming. That young man, who pulled the branch from the rosebush with his bare and bleeding hand, was a business major. But now, he is Fr. Mick Kelly of the Arlington, Virginia diocese – one of two men we know who became priests as a result of Brian's death.

But what about Terrell and Nathan, the two young men who took Brian's and Aaron's lives? I'm sure Brian and Aaron want them to know the joy of Christianity. We pray for them every day. We pray that they realize what they did. They took two innocent human lives, and justice demands they be punished for the rest of their lives because life is that valuable. But mercy demands that we love them, and help them see that they can make their lives in prison their path to heaven.

In our culture, we have to be radical witnesses of life. We must stand up for all life and say that all life is precious: the unborn, the elderly, the handicapped, the poor, and yes, the criminal.

During the trials, we had to drive to the courthouse in Steubenville, and we would see little children standing at the bus stop. I would think, "Maybe Nathan and Terrell stood at that very bus stop when they were little boys." They were not born killers. They became killers. Why? We learned at the trials that they had no fathers. They had older brothers who sold drugs, used drugs, and hurt people. Their mothers were in and out of jail and prison for all kinds of various reasons.

Terrell and Nathan were little troublemakers when they were boys, and then they became bullies at school. Eventually, they stopped going to school altogether, and no one noticed. No one cared. So they began doing what their older brothers were doing: selling drugs, using drugs, and hurting people. I thought, "What can we do to help children like them?" I know there are children growing up like that in every city in America.

That's why we started what we call the Run the Race Club on the west side of Columbus — the most violent neighborhood in the city. It's a world where parents aren't and never have been married, where drugs reign supreme, where the dropout rate is almost 40%, and those who stay in school are in substandard schools. The children are always hungry. They have lice and bedbugs. They live with mice and rats. They are not at grade level in reading or math, and they have never been in any church.

We gathered them together for meals, tutoring, crafts, games, Bible stories, sports, and more. All these activities were vehicles through which we built relationships with them and loved them. And what do our children suffer from the most? Moral poverty. The scars left by moral poverty manifest as a lack of impulse control and empathy, and without these, a child's loneliness and hunger turn to bitterness. That bitterness turns to anger, and that unholy anger eventually explodes — usually on an innocent person like Brian. So, we see each Run the Race child as a child of God who has been treated very badly and needs real love to heal. And we learn what real love is from Jesus Christ.

We learn that the essence of love is to give oneself to the other. Jesus does this; He is not possessive of His divinity or His abilities. That is why He gives Himself so fully in the Holy Eucharist. He gives His Body, Blood, Soul, and Divinity. All the virtues in Him, He gives to us. All the wisdom in Him, He gives to us. All the grace in Him, He gives to us. "If only you knew the gift of God," Jesus says to the Samaritan woman. He says it to us, too. If only we knew that God seeks every possible means to share by grace what He possesses by nature, and He does it for our sake because He loves us.

So, what is the antidote to the coldness, hatred, violence, and crassness in our society today? It's love — real love. Unselfish acts of true kindness are God's remedies to our problems. Real love never gives up on anyone. Real love is kindness, forgiveness, justice, and mercy, all wrapped up together. Real love brings peace of heart, joy, and unity. And we can see real love because it was made visible in Jesus Christ, the God-man, who shows us what it's like to be fully human — who asks questions and demands decisions that challenge us to the depths of our souls.

A Jesus who says, "Whatever you do is okay," is a fiction. The Jesus of the Gospels is demanding, bold, and lovable. So, do you have someone to forgive? Please, forgive them. Do you need forgiveness? Be bold, be brave, and ask for it. You won't regret it.

I want to close by giving thanks to God for a great gift — the gift of everlasting life. I know Brian lives because he lived in Christ during his short 18 years on earth. Live your life in Christ, and you can change the world. God bless you. [*audience applause*]

McCarthy: In the spirit of this moment, I'm going to ask for forgiveness instead of permission by going off script. The program has me offering some concluding remarks, but after what we just heard, I'd be an idiot to try to conclude. None of us have any business concluding. We shouldn't be concluding now. What we should do, I submit, is mull over what we've heard. Bear it in mind. Keep it in heart. Think about it. Reflect on it. Ponder what Leo Schofield has lived through for 36 years. If you listen to that podcast, you'll hear Leo's voice. He tells the truth, and Leo's humanity comes through intensely in the words he speaks to Gilbert.

Ponder what Rachel has gone through. Imagine yourself in the situations they've lived through. Recollect it. Let them be examples for you. And I'm preaching this to myself before I say anything to you. It's surely obvious that the forgiveness — the remarkable acts of forgiveness — that we've just heard about could not have occurred in the absence of hope. The hopeless are simply incapable of forgiving. Forgiveness is, in fact, among the greatest expressions of hope.

This brings me to the second part of the script I refuse to follow. Our friend — our dear friend — Angelo, sitting right here, asked me to respond now to the question, "Is hope possible?" To that question, any one of us could and should answer, "Of course it is," because we've seen it. We see hope in Leo, in Rachel, and in many other people we've met or heard about over this weekend.

I'm going to say just a little about what hope is, but that means first saying something about what it is not. When we say to a friend who's sick,

"I hope you feel better soon," we don't really mean it. It's possible that when we say such things, we feel bad that our friend is ill, and it's possible that we genuinely want them to get better. But we don't truly invest hope in that desire. Why should we? Most of the time, we're pretty sure they will get better. Hope isn't the point. Hope is not merely a desire, and it's not at all like optimism.

The optimist says, "It'll all be okay." And the hysterically optimistic person says, "It'll all get better really soon." But however well-meaning those who talk that way may be, if that's what they always say, they're either always lying or always thoughtless. Leo's wife and Rachel's son were both murdered. They are not ever coming home. Ever. To say to Leo, "It'll all be better," doesn't change the 36 years that are gone. Hope is also not the stuff of a sports movie – though those often follow the arc of the underdog's triumph after a wearisome series of crushing defeats.

Hope is not the bracing cheer of "We can do this!" from a beleaguered band confident in its own powers. Peguy, I think, put it best. These are God's words, according to Peguy: "The faith I love best," says God, "is hope. Faith doesn't surprise me – it's not surprising. Charity," says God, "that doesn't surprise me. But hope", says God, "that is something that surprises me – even me." That is surprising: that these poor children see how things are going and still believe that tomorrow things will get better. That they see how things are today and believe that they will get better tomorrow morning. That is surprising, and it's by far the greatest marvel of our grace."

So then, Peguy likens hope to a little girl who tugs between her two sisters, Faith and Charity. The little girl is certainly confident, but the confidence is decidedly not in herself. Nor does she hope to have an exact picture of where she's headed or where she will end up.

For over three decades, Leo has hoped that his innocence and the dreadful time for which he was wrongfully convicted would be recognized by the law. For all he knew, that might not have happened, and yet, Leo carried on in hope. For all these years, Rachel has hoped that the killers of her son would recognize what they've done, lament it, repent, and that hasn't happened yet.

To liken hope to a tireless little girl should not lead us to think that hope is naive. Leo, Rachel, Arvo Pärt, Monsignor Albacete when he was with us, Cardinal Pizzaballa, and many others we've heard about these past days are not naive people. They are not shallow. If hope were a function of stupidity or naivete, it would quickly peter out. The hard realities of life put an end to those who mistake pleasant dreams and idle fantasies for hope.

What distinguishes wishful thinking from the hope of those who hope in the ways we've seen over these days? What's the difference? Pope Benedict XVI in his *Spe Salvi* and Father Luigi Giussani in his *Is It Possible to Live This Way?* both emphasize something surprising about hope: its certainty. Hope is in no way a crapshoot. The source of that certainty, they both insist, is not just something up ahead where we hope to land; it's not something only behind us, but something present now — evident, palpable, real.

The little girl, Hope, charges ahead. She doesn't just patiently suffer the burdens of life because of her confidence in the good that governs her life. In the midst of whatever she must bear right now, she can't draw with any precision the contours of the good that lies ahead of her, but somehow she knows that the good that embraces her in the moment will continue to embrace her, that it's up ahead, waiting eagerly, reaching out to her.

That's what hope is. And what about the rest of us? Peguy says this about hope: "To hope, my child, you'd have to be quite fortunate, to have received a great grace." We're not, I dare say, very good at hope nowadays; we're not great hopers. But we can catch glimpses of it in others, and we can want it for ourselves. Can we hope to be hopeful? I don't know. What we can do is put ourselves in the company of those who hope when we see them, when we recognize them. So I invite you to do that. Stay in the company of Rachel, in the company of Leo through Gilbert. Wherever you see it, follow it.

Thank you. [*audience applause*]

www.ingramcontent.com/pod-product-compliance
Lightning Source LLC
Chambersburg PA
CBHW061651040426
42446CB00010B/1687